MANAGEMENT SKILLS IN SOCIAL CARE

To Bobbie, Karl, Lydia, Seth and Vicky: our long-suffering partners and children.

Management Skills in Social Care

A handbook for social care managers

John Harris
Des Kelly

First published in hardback by Gower Publishing Company Limited.

This edition published by
Ashgate
Ashgate Publishing Limited
Gower House
Croft Road
Aldershot
Hants GU11 3HR
England

Ashgate Publishing Company
Old Post Road
Brookfield
Vermont 05036
USA

British Library Cataloguing in Publication Data
Harris, John, *1952-*
    Management skills in social care: a handbook for social care managers.
    1. Great Britain. Welfare work. Management
    I. Title   II. Kelly, Des, *1952-*
    361.3068

Library of Congress Cataloguing in Publication Data
Harris, John, *1952-*
    Management skills in social care: a handbook for social care managers.
    John Harris, Des Kelly.
       p. cm.
    1. Social work administration.   I. Kelly, Desmond.   II. Title.
    HV40.H32 1990
    361'.0068-dc20   90-38652
                                                          CIP

ISBN: 1 85742 081 0

Printed in Great Britain by
Billing & Sons Ltd, Worcester

Contents

Foreword

The Report *Residential Care: A Positive Choice* recommended that all senior posts in residential care should be filled by staff with social work qualifications by 1993. Apart from anything else the lack of available training places means that this recommendation will not be implemented in the near future, although it remains as a challenge. But even if it could be implemented how many of those senior staff would have had the kind of 'hands on' management training this handbook provides?

The Handbook for Social Care Managers entitled Management Skills in Social Care comes at a time when the lessons it has to teach are sorely needed. The crucial role that good social care managers play is coming to be better understood and appreciated. They are the people who set the tone in social care settings and whose influence can enhance the quality of life of service users. But when do they have the time and where can they go to learn the skills they need?

Management Skills in Social Care is written in a clear direct style that makes it easy reading. It is full of practical suggestions for improving the management techniques of both new managers and those who are already in management roles. Its 'do it yourself' style involves the reader directly and provides her with a rough and ready assessment of her performance.

Managers are very often promoted on the strength of competence as practitioners with little or no guidance on how to tackle their new responsibilities. I very much welcome this attempt to fill a widely felt gap. I am sure Management Skills in Social Care will appeal to a wide variety of professionals who have management responsibilities both inside the residential care sector and in the wider social care field.

Lady Gillian Wagner
Chair of the Independent
Review of Residential Care

Preface

This is a *practice-based handbook*. It has emerged from our experiences as managers and from our reflections on those experiences, and it is rooted in the reader's experience of the issues which it tackles. It is a *handbook* rather than a book about management theories. It is to management what a recipe book is to cooking. Just as in a recipe book you can look up boiling an egg or cooking a three-course meal, but you will search in vain for a discussion of the physics of conducted heat, so in this handbook you can look up running a staff meeting or team development but you will search in vain for a learned discussion of management theory. You may, of course, decide to modify a particular recipe!

We were originally convinced of the need for such a handbook by the growing recognition of the importance of management in the personal social services, alongside the relative neglect of management in residential and day care settings which existed up to a few years ago. The book began as a response to this neglect. However our experience of working with many managers from the public, private and voluntary sectors and from a variety of service settings has led us to extend our remit to social care more generally. In the main the content of the book reflects this shift towards a wider audience, while still retaining our initial concern for residential and day care services.

The book also had its origins in our awareness of managers often being promoted on the basis of their competence as practitioners and then feeling ill-equipped to embrace the problems and possibilities offered by a management position. As a practice-based handbook emphasis is laid on ways in which managers of social care provision can improve their expertise. As such, we think that it has something to offer to newly-appointed managers, to practitioners who are considering the possibility of a management post and to managers already in post who want to review their performance. It may be helpful to the supervisors of managers in social care settings, to advisers linked to these services and to educators and trainers. In addition, the content of much of the book could be usefully applied to the management of field social work services.

How you make use of the book will, to some extent, depend on which of the above categories you fall into. The book can be worked through in detail in order to come to grips with the overall scope of a particular managerial post or it can be dipped into as a source of easily accessible information on specific topics. Hints on using the material are provided at the beginning of each chapter. Throughout the book you will be invited in self-directed *activities* to reflect on your experience, to think through issues, to take part in exercises, to contemplate doing things differently. We urge you to accept these invitations when you come across them. We firmly believe that adults learn effectively when they are actively involved in their own development. We have deliberately adopted a format which facilitates self-assessment and which enables you to personalize the book's subject matter. This type of format is also used as a way of dealing with both the range and size of settings in which readers work. We cannot address the detailed way in which such factors affect your job. Using the activities we have included in the book, you can.

There is much talk about the quality of the service provided in social care settings but high-quality care seldom just happens. It has to be managed. Accordingly, this book stresses the contribution of management. As such it does not address direct practice with service users. Nevertheless we believe that effective management is essential to the improvement of day-to-day practice. The book stems from our belief that management matters.

John Harris
Des Kelly

Acknowledgements

There are a number of people to whom we are grateful for their help in enabling this book finally to be produced:

People on the receiving end of services for which we have been responsible.

Colleagues we have worked with in a range of settings.

Managers who have been subjected to our ideas on a series of Social Care Association courses; these courses have enabled us to test out our thinking and refine our ideas and their presentation.

Bobbie, Karl, Lydia, Seth and Vicky, for their support and their tolerance of our nocturnal absences while writing this book.

Joan and Karen who have struggled with the typing of successive drafts as the manuscript took shape and Peter for managing the intricacies of the word processor.

Needless to say we have learned a great deal from others over the years, but the responsibility for what follows, as always, rests with us.

1 Social care management in transition

How to read this chapter. . .

Most of this chapter may be regarded initially as a 'take-it-or-leave-it' chapter! It sets the scene for consideration of the personal transition to management in social care settings in the context of a brief summary of historical developments and recent trends. It is intended that the reader who has experienced the rapid rate of change and its consequences will find the chapter useful in untangling some of the themes and issues. It is therefore a general introduction to which some readers may wish to return at a later point. However, unlike many of the following chapters, it is not for dipping into or using selected sections, with the exception of the final section 'moving on to management' (p. 7) which should be considered before tackling the rest of the book.

Contexts: past and present

The images of social care have their roots in the prison, the work-house and the asylum (Parker, 1988). These images have proved remarkably resistant to change despite the fact that the functions of social care have altered substantially. The concept of the 'total institution' (Goffman 1968), for example, which has been so influential on the development of residential services, has probably been over-stated and yet it remains a powerful image which is often seen as typifying service provision. The institutional images of social care

1

services in the public and professional mind impinge on the task of managing these resources. The images easily become stereotyped into a perception of social care as the poor relation within the personal social services. In addition, the status of social care work can be seen as simply reflecting the ambivalent attitude towards what is regarded as 'women's work', of caring, nurturing and tending within the wider society. For managers this ambivalence about social care may form part of the context of much of their working life.

The pace of change within the personal social services in general quickened from 1970 onwards. Within social care the pace of change has been quite dramatic. The distribution of services has shifted across statutory, voluntary and private provision, culminating in the development of a mixed economy of welfare (Department of Health, 1989). A series of apparent alternatives to residential and day care provision have developed in response to a combination of perceived needs and economic constraints. Family placement now provides substitute 'families' for the full range of service users. Independent living, sheltered housing, changes in the functions of the home care service, core and cluster developments and group homes have given services a different complexion and have challenged previously sacrosanct arrangements. These changes have been accompanied by new thinking and new practices, particularly in relation to the management of services.

Social care services have developed in this contradictory climate. They have changed and survived. They have continued to be a major resource in local authorities. They have grown steadily in the voluntary sphere and they have expanded quite dramatically in the private sector. However, at the same time, criticisms of regimes, institutionalized practices and adverse effects on clients have continued to be researched and reported. (Wagner Vol. II, 1988). Residential care particularly, continues to be seen as essential and marginal at the same time – in demand and yet a last resort!

An examination of the development of social care suggests that the principles of social work advocated for the fieldwork sector have been taken over and rather loosely applied, with limited success. This has contributed to patchy and inconsistent services, with inappropriate practices and thwarted developments, as provision directed at resolving accommodation and/or social problems has given way to services attempting to meet a complex mix of social, emotional and physical needs. Developments in field social work, particularly in relation to the policy of community care, have not been realized to the full as financial restrictions have constrained growth, but the policy has nevertheless contributed to a fundamental questioning of the role of social care provision and has resulted in cuts in building programmes. Gradually staff have experienced the implications of these changes: child care has come to mean working with difficult adolescents; family centres are increasingly presented with multiple problems; day nurseries confront the sensitive and potentially explosive situation of child abuse in its many forms; the policy of deinstitutionalization in the field of mental health has placed additional stress on social care services; the growth in the numbers of older people and in the proportion deemed in need of care has increased in real terms, which has led to claims of greater levels of dependency in social care establishments; developments in community care, particularly the 'staying put' initiatives, have also led directly to substantial changes in the use and role of social care services. The result of these interrelated trends has been experienced by many social care staff as a process of forceful and rapid change to which provision is constantly having to adapt.

In this rapidly changing context, serious consideration of management activity within the personal social services developed slowly but is now well established at least in relation to senior and middle managers (Department of Health, 1990). The work of the Audit Commission in promoting the 3Es – efficiency, effectiveness, economics – has emphasized the importance of management expertise across the range of settings in the personal social services. The publication of the Wagner and Griffiths Reports (1988) and the White Paper, *Caring for People* (1989) served to reinforce the central contribution of management in social care settings in ways which are likely to ensure that it remains centre stage for the foreseeable future. Accordingly, many senior staff will have experienced their job title being changed in ways which attempt to reflect a new managerial emphasis. These changes in job titles symbolize an era of change. Matron, Superintendent and Warden have given way to Officer-in-Charge, Head of Home, Principal Residential Social Worker and, more recently, Residential Manager, Unit Manager, Centre Manager, with corresponding posts at deputy and assistant levels. Job advertisements have certainly reflected this change of emphasis, which is part of a process of trying to enhance the management of services.

Social care management has some unique aspects and makes particular demands. For senior staff it means managing 'teams' of staff who share day-to-day reponsibility for service users, often in the context of having shift patterns on a rostered basis. It is likely that managers will also work shifts which involve, in the residential sector, a mixture of early mornings, evenings, nights and sleeping-in duties. There can be few managers in other occupations who are expected to be able to weld together aspects of social care, social work, nursing, catering, hotelling, personnel practice, industrial relations, administration and finance. At the same time social care managers are also required to rise above the pressures inherent in these individual activities in order to generate values and attitudes which result in services being closely aligned to the needs of clients.

The impact of the changes we have outlined on management posts and the particular demands of social care settings have been amplified by a further extension in the manager's role: managers have increasingly been charged with the additional responsibility of introducing and carrying out change. In many organizations this requirement has been accompanied by downward shifts in levels of managerial responsibility, so that much of the daily work of managers now involves the process of coordinating a range of diverse activities in the context of wider change.

The future promises to be equally challenging, as new tasks and responsibilities emerge. The National Vocational Qualifications framework, for example, will require social care managers to adopt a high profile in relation to training and assessing staff.

Social care managers should also be in the forefront of developing anti-discriminatory policies and practices over the next few years. Although within social care settings there are some examples of vigorous attention to equal opportunities and anti-discriminatory practice, much social care provision has been on the sidelines of attempts to move forward on these fronts. This is beginning to change (see, for example, S.C.A. 1990). Some of the material in this book can be used to advance these issues. For example, we have worked with managers in promoting equal opportunities and developing anti-discriminatory practice using the material in the final chapter on Managing Change. Chapter 7 on Training can similarly be used to address these issues with individual staff.

What do we mean by management?

Drucker (1975) states that managers set goals and objectives, organize tasks to meet the objectives set, communicate and motivate, monitor and evaluate, develop people and teams and delegate. Lawrence identifies four key elements of management which we find useful:

- Getting things done with people
- Setting objectives
- Taking decisions about the means by which objectives will be reached
- Solving problems which frustrate the achievement of objectives.

(Lawrence, 1986, pp. 2–3)

The problem with such definitions of management, as Lawrence recognizes, is that they can imply that management is an activity distinctly different from other activities. However, if we think about the way we use the term 'managing' in everyday speech – 'managing to do the gardening/reading/cooking' – the ordinariness of the act of 'managing' becomes immediately obvious. Similarly, if we take an example from a social care setting, a residential social worker in a children's centre 'manages' the task of getting a group of children up, washed, dressed and off to school – and a great deal else besides! Therefore, in emphasizing 'management', all we are doing is stressing the content of a more explicitly managerial post with elements which may be every bit as mundane as those in many other jobs. This notion of management does not conform to the popular stereotype of management as a detached, orderly, rational activity of great authority and status, or worse, of management as the province of a macho elite. In this respect Mount's (1977) distinction between to manage in French as *ménager*, managing as in the running of a household, and in Italian as *maneggiare*, as in handling horses, is useful. *Maneggiare* has been the dominant conception of management. Unfortunately much of the management literature clouds the ordinariness of aspects of '*ménager*' by obscuring the obvious and ordinary in exhortations to embrace a macho management style!

Is this book for you?

Despite more attention being paid to management, the popular notion that it is something picked up on becoming a manager is still much in evidence in social care settings. This notion is reinforced in the residential sector by the rapid movement of newly qualified staff into senior positions. There is a debate about whether basic qualifying training in social work should encompass preparation for management responsibilities. Within social care, basic training is often the *only* preparation for managerial responsibility and this reinforces the view that good practitioners make good managers – if you are good at a job you will naturally be good at managing someone else doing the same job! Although we are convinced that practitioners can carry over skills into managerial positions, we consider that it cannot be taken for granted that managing is something which comes naturally to good practitioners. Many of the people who become social care managers may not be comfortable with the traditional male-dominated image of management, which emphasizes competitiveness, aggression and authoritarianism. White women and black men and women may encounter particular barriers to the establishing of a style of management which is acceptable to them, especially if they find themselves isolated within a hostile management culture.

Nevertheless, the struggle to develop an approach to management is important. The rejection of a view of management as the arbitrary and authoritarian imposition of a manager's will, and the failure to develop alternative approaches, has led some managers in social care settings to conclude that there is no room for 'management' at all. In some circumstances where managers have accepted the status of manager but abdicated managerial responsibility a vacuum has emerged which at best has been filled by a well-meaning, amiable chaos and at worst by a collusive, oppressive staff culture which has exploited users, as witnessed by a succession of scandals.

This book will fill some of the gaps a practitioner may discover on becoming a manager. It provides information and guidance on principles and techniques to which a new manager, or a manager wishing to review her practice, can turn. These principles and techniques are primarily applied to the management of social care services, although it is likely that they could be used equally effectively in other settings such as fieldwork. We hope that the book will also serve as a starting-point for people considering senior positions in social care, as well as enabling existing senior staff to reflect on their role, the tasks associated with it and the ways in which it has changed and will continue to change. The book, then, seeks to point a way forward in an area that has not been well signposted for social care managers.

Some readers may be preoccupied at the outset with our emphasis on management and in particular may query whether they actually are managers. Within social care it is possible to find many staff in senior positions who do not have the word 'manager' in their title. Nevertheless, the absence of the word does not necessarily mean the absence of the managerial role. You may be in charge of a group of staff. As their supervisor you will have the right to make decisions and to give guidance about areas of work in which you were previously a recipient of decisions. However you will not be entirely free to 'do your own thing'. You will have a supervisor, who in turn will be answerable to another tier in the management structure. In your supervisory role you have the responsibility to achieve at least an adequate standard of service for clients. This service will be achieved through the efforts of the people for whom you are responsible. Their value and potential contribution should not be underestimated nor taken for granted. This supervisory responsibility is a major part of a managerial role and, used well, it brings the opportunity for maximizing the potential of the service provided by the staff.

Moving on to management

Everything we have discussed so far points to social care management being in a state of transition. This is not simply interesting, rather it has major implications for holders of management posts.

Moving on to a management post is in itself a transition which can represent a major life change. It is often a mixture of excitement at the challenge offered by new opportunities and anxiety about whether expectations can be met. It is likely to be associated with feelings about leaving others behind, isolation, even betrayal, as much as a boost to confidence and career prospects.

Many managers find that the transition to a new post follows the sort of pattern we have set out in Figure 1.1. A new manager may have been pushed or pulled towards a new job by various factors: pushed, for instance, by dissatisfaction with aspects of a previous job, or pulled by aspects of their present post; status, more money, a feeling that the job could be done at least as well as it is by some of the other people in posts at that level! Getting the new job may have been a high spot, only to be followed by a sense of anticlimax when work in the new post began, as the constraints and difficulties moved into the foreground. Being able to emerge from this trough to the point at which the reality of the job, positive and negative, can be dealt with is, it is hoped, the point managers finally reach.

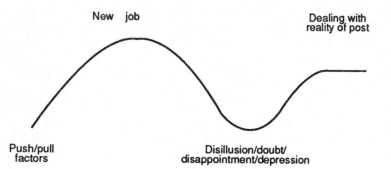

New job

Dealing with reality of post

Push/pull factors

Disillusion/doubt/ disappointment/depression

Figure 1.1   Transition to a management post.

It is important to acknowledge the way in which the general trends and wider issues we have outlined exert a force on individual managers. The effects of personal change also need to be understood in helping managers deal with their new roles and responsibilities. Successfully coping with the transition to management is the only way that new managers can become effective managers.

The following chapters unpick some of the complexity of general trends and personal change in relation to specific elements of the manager's job in social care. Readers will be aided by exercises which attempt to make the text specific to their work settings. You are invited to start this process by answering the questions in the activity below.

The ability of managers to cope with the transition to a new post will depend on a number of factors:

- knowing themselves,
- knowing the new situation,
- sources of support,
- looking after themselves,
- leaving the past behind,
- looking for benefits.

Activity: self-audit

A useful starting-point in thinking about your work as a manager is to undertake a self-audit by answering the following questions:

1. Look back at the material on *general* developments in management (pp. 1–4). Have they affected you? If so, how?
2. (a) Within social care, in which particular sector do you work?
   (b) With which user group do you work?
   (c) What developments have there been in your *specific* area of work which affect your management role?
3. What were the personal implications of the move into your present management post?
4. Using the headings below, identify the assets you have in your present circumstances.

Knowing yourself
Knowing the situation
Sources of support
Looking after yourself
Leaving the past behind
Looking for benefits

2 Managing yourself

How to read this chapter. . .

Management is often thought of in terms of managing the work of others, of 'getting things done through people'. However, in order to be an effective manager, it is also necessary to be able to manage yourself.

The main purpose of this chapter is to introduce the idea of managing yourself. How can you obtain the maximum use of yourself as a resource? Of course the response you make to this question will be a personal one; you ought to be the best person to judge how you manage yourself.

If this is the first attempt you have made to consider the idea of self-management, we suggest that you work through this chapter systematically. Alternatively, if you want to brush up on specific areas of self-management, turn to the sections on:

Planning
Deciding priorities
Managing time
Leadership style
Dealing with stress
Delegation.

Activity

Before you begin, consider the descriptions of managers given below, which suggest a number of ways in which you can judge how well a manager manages herself. Read them through and choose which is the most important standard for judging whether a manager manages herself well. Tick the *one* which you think is the most important.

1. She is always busy.
2. She takes work home.
3. She can always get away promptly from work.
4. Her members of staff work harder than she does.
5. She gets the desired results in the available time.
6. She does not waste other people's time.
7. She is always ready to help.
8. She makes it difficult for other people to interrupt her.
9. She is always in the office early.
10. She is a good leader.
11. She makes decisions quickly.
12. She has stamina for continuous hard work.

Comments

1. × Is she busy doing the right things?
2. × Many managers do. Some are good and some are bad at managing themselves.
3. × But this could be a good sign if she is getting the job done.
4. × But she is probably good at delegation!
5. √
6. × She may be wasting her own time if she does not know what she should be doing.
7. × But she is nice to have around.
8. × Building barriers is a technique which can be used, but is she getting results?
9. × She may be desperate to get away from home!
10. × Nevertheless, leadership is important to a manager.
11. × You save time in decision-making by making the *right* decision first time.
12. × Stamina is invaluable – particularly if she is *not* managing herself well.

(Adapted from Colt Training Aids (1972) Self-management Programme.)

Although many of the other characteristics may be desirable in managers they are only a means to an end, not an end in themselves.

Planning

In a study of managing directors, Carlson (1951) found that most had between 34 and 40 different things to do in a typical day, each lasting between 3 and 20 minutes. None of the managing directors had an uninterrupted period in which to reflect on their philosophy of management or their policies. All of them were without long-range plans for their work. Mintzberg (1973) found that the main characteristics of managerial work were brevity, variety and fragmentation. As yet there are no comparable 'classic' studies of managers of social care. However our experience suggests that the content of managers' work in social care settings is similar to that found in the studies mentioned. The nature of managerial work, combined with failure to plan, can set up a vicious circle in which the absence of planning becomes a reason for the absence of planning.

It is important that the attitude that it is a poor use of time to sit, think and plan should be dispelled, particularly for new managers. There can be little doubt that time spent on planning actually saves time. The maxim of doing first things first is essential to this. Reserving some time at the beginning or end of each day can be a productive way of ensuring that adequate forward planning will enable the most effective use of yourself, on a day-to-day basis. Building set review periods into your work and that of any other managers in your service is also a useful means of encouraging planning and review in the longer term.

Activity

If you decide to act on either of the suggestions made above, that is, reserving time and setting review periods, try making a list of your current priorities on a daily and longer-term basis. Implement the suggestion(s) and then compare your initial notes with the priorities which emerge.

Deciding priorities

If you take the planning component of your role as a manager seriously you will encounter the need to make priorities. Deciding on priorities, making conscious choices about the importance you attach to certain issues, may lead to conflict with other issues vying for your attention. There are three common sources of conflict.

Firstly, conflicts can exist *between* priorities. For example, training may be considered important, but the consequence may be a temporary reduction in the amount of work it is possible to complete. Secondly, conflicts may emerge *within* a priority area of work. For example, is it more important to get a particular job finished on time or to achieve a high-quality result? Thirdly, conflicts can develop between *short- and longer-term* priorities. For example, a decision may be taken on the short-term organization of an individual staff member's role which establishes an awkward precedent or has damaging consequences for the motivation of other staff.

In deciding on priorities it is essential that potentially competing priorities are kept in balance. The time-scale for decision-making is the main control. For social care managers time-scales will often be tight. The danger is that, given such time constraints, managers may fall for the lure of 'crisis management' and simply tumble from one problem situation to another. It may be worth remembering that wrong decisions made about people can lead to years of management effort being necessary to overcome poor morale or a bad atmosphere. Scott and Rochester (1984) suggest the following time-scale for priorities:

Decisions in which the priority is *work* generally need little lead-time. They can be quickly implemented and the results are soon evident. Decisions in which the priority is *money* usually require longer lead-times to implement. It may take several months before the efforts produce the desired results. Decisions in which *people*'s attitudes, abilities and working relationships are the priority take the longest lead-times. It may take years of work to achieve the intended results. (See Chapter 8 for a more detailed account of this aspect of the management role).

Activity

Reflect on a recent difficult decision on priorities which you had to make. Use the material above to analyse the *source* of the conflict in priorities and the *time-scale* needed to implement the priority you chose.

DECISION	SOURCE OF CONFLICTING PRIORITIES	TIME-SCALE FOR IMPLEMENTATION

Managing time

As you begin consciously to address the question of determining time-scales, you will be brought face to face with your attitudes towards the use of time. In some social care settings, as in many other workplaces, there is great emphasis on being busy. There is no automatic relationship between apparent hard work and positive accomplishment. A flurry of activity does not necessarily achieve the best results. Indeed the inability of a manager to organize herself, because there is always something else more important to do, can be indicative of insecurity about what would be done, if only time were available. Barrett (1977) suggests that there are different levels of ability to manage time:

- nothing planned/time unorganized;
- recognition that time is a resource;
- budgeting time: specific periods for specific tasks;
- future planning: forecasting demands on time;
- goal-directed use of time: making the future happen.

It is not easy to become 'goal-directed'. Being busy *is* a problem. All managers of social care provision have externally imposed constraints which keep them busy. All the more reason, then, to come to terms with self-generated factors which further militate against good management of time. Such factors can include:

- attempting too much at once,
- unrealistic time estimates,

- lack of organization,
- failure to listen,
- doing something yourself, which could properly be done by someone else.

If any of this is even partly true for you, you may want to change your practice to gain more control over the way you use your time.

For example, having an ever-open door is sometimes the proud boast of social care managers. Used indiscriminately, such a practice can be counter-productive to managerial effectiveness. Constant interruptions prevent planning, distract attention and fuel the belief that it is impossible to organize work with people on a planned basis. Always being available can, in addition, have the unfortunate consequence of fostering dependency in staff. The 'ever-open door' approach can actually invite interruptions and it can lead to a manager's unnecessary involvement in detailed decisions. These disadvantages can be obscured by the bustle of the daily melée of social care life. The 'ever-open door' will be perceived as such, and the managerial role will be reduced to directing traffic at a busy crossroads! Staff effectiveness will also be impaired if the manager is successful in conveying the message that simply being busy is effective management of time. Involvement in detailed decisions may feel satisfying to managers but it will stunt staff development and hinder good use of staff time. Here are some ideas for better habits!

- reserving a quiet hour at the beginning of the day;
- arriving early rather than staying late;
- having a separate room or office for tasks that require concentration or privacy;
- keeping the door open for periods of the day and closed when you wish to signify that interruptions are not welcome (this could include telephone interruptions and other distractions);
- the use of screening, for example, by a clerk or junior staff in an attempt to order subsequent work;
- establishing a system of set times for supervision sessions and other predictable commitments, and keeping to them;
- drawing up a list of the activities you want to engage in during the next month(s). Decide in which week action will be needed on each of the activities. Allocate time to the action required.

Unplanned activities should then be competing for a smaller proportion of your time.

Activity

Under the headings given below, make two lists, 'How I waste my time' and 'How other people waste my time' and make some suggestions of ways in which some of the time-wasting, under both headings, can be dealt with.

How I Waste My Time	Suggestions for Improvement	How Other People Waste My Time	Suggestions for Improvement

Leadership style

Activity

Work through the statements below, which consist of management assumptions about people. Place a tick against one from each of the pairs of statements, according to which statement most closely reflects your assumptions about people.

1. (a) It is only human nature to do as little work as possible.
   (b) People only avoid work when their work has been deprived of meaning.
2. (a) People with access to more information than they need for their immediate tasks usually misuse it.
   (b) People with access to any information they want behave responsibly.
3. (a) Expecting people to make useful suggestions about their work is a waste of time because their perspective is limited.
   (b) Asking people for their ideas broadens their perspective and results in useful suggestions.
4. (a) People do not show imagination and ingenuity at work because most people have little of either.
   (b) Most people are imaginative and creative but do not show it

because of the limitations imposed by their managers and by the job.

5. (a) People who are not reprimanded for all of their mistakes tend to lower their standards.

   (b) People who are responsible for their own work and for putting right their own mistakes tend to raise their standards.

6. (a) People should only be told good news, as bad news will have an adverse effect on their work.

   (b) People want to know all about the affairs of the organization, both good and bad.

7. (a) A manager should never admit to a member of staff that she was wrong as it will lower her prestige.

   (b) The prestige of the manager is increased when she admits a mistake.

8. (a) Those allowed to set their own targets and standards set them lower than their manager would.

   (b) Those allowed to set their own targets and standards set them higher than their manager would.

9. (a) The more knowledge and freedom a member of staff has about her job, the more controls are needed to keep her in line.

   (b) The more knowledge and freedom a member of staff has about her job, the fewer controls are needed.

(Now carry on reading. We will return to the activity in due course.)

We all have views on how we should be led. These views influence how we think we should lead other people. Leadership is an important issue. We should not lose sight of the importance of leadership. A service can be well managed but may still not achieve its full potential if there is dissatisfaction with a manager's leadership style. McGregor (1960) suggests that leadership style develops from our basic attitudes and assumptions about people. He sets out this proposition by highlighting two contrasting sets of assumptions which he calls 'Theory X' and 'Theory Y'.

THEORY X

1. The average human being has an inherent dislike of work and will avoid it.

2. Because of this dislike of work, most people must be coerced, closely supervised, directed or threatened with punishment to get them to work hard or, alternatively, financially bribed.

3. The average human being prefers to be directed, wishes to avoid responsibility and has relatively little ambition.

THEORY Y

1. The expenditure of physical and mental effort in work is as natural as play or rest; work may be a source of satisfaction and can be voluntarily performed.
2. The threat of punishment and close supervision are not the only means of making people work reasonably hard. People will exercise self-direction and self-control when working for something to which they are committed.
3. Commitment to a job can be obtained if the individual gains a sense of satisfaction, achievement and self-esteem in carrying out the work.
4. The average human being learns, under proper conditions, not only to accept, but to seek responsibility.

(Adapted from Douglas McGregor, 1960.)

Look back at the activity. The 'a' statements were based on Theory X assumptions, the 'b' statements were based on Theory Y assumptions. Did you lean more towards a Theory X or Theory Y style of leadership? Peters and Waterman (1982) suggest that 'most organisations are governed by rules that assume the average worker is an incompetent ne'er-do-well just itching to screw up' (Theory X). They found that successful companies, 'treat people as adults. Treat people as partners; treat them with dignity; treat them with respect' (Theory Y). McGregor suggests that leaders with Theory Y assumptions encourage innovation in their staff, achieve better results and have fewer incidents of conflict.

You may or may not share these views about leadership. You may have found yourself mentally nodding as you read the above, or disagreeing violently. Think about your reactions, and try to sum up your assumptions about people, and what they mean for the leadership style which you try to employ. We would argue strongly for authenticity. If you lean towards 'X' leadership, but constantly tell staff that you operate on a 'Y' basis, you will produce frustration and confusion. Think about the sort of leader you are. Do you want to change any aspects of your leadership style? If not, accept it!

This emphasis on a personal leadership style which stems from our assumptions about people is one part of the equation. The other part is the situation in which the manager finds herself. Leadership style is shaped by external pressures as well as internal assumptions. For example, the agency may have developed a socially sanctioned preference for a particular leadership style. However, given the amount of day-to-day autonomy enjoyed by most social care managers, personal leadership style may be more influential than it is for managers in many other settings. Nevertheless the style of leadership which emerges will, to some extent, be the outcome of the interplay between personal preference and the situation faced by the manager.

We have represented this interplay in diagrammatic form below (Figure 2.1) as a means of charting influences on a manager's leadership style. If you worked through the factors we have identified with another manager, the extent to which the interplay between each manager's work situation and personal preferences throws up a particular style of leadership would become clear.

One way of categorizing styles of leadership is by drawing a distinction between the amount of direction (task) and the amount of support (relationship) that a leader should provide, given the

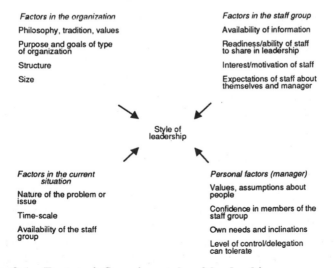

Figure 2.1 Factors influencing style of leadership.

work situation and the staff group. *Task behaviour* on the part of the manager involves one-way communication to staff. The manager explains what to do and how to do it. *Relationship behaviour* involves two-way communication, in which the manager provides support to staff in determining their approach to their work. As staff become capable of accomplishing specific tasks, the leadership style is less focused on task, and more attuned to relationships. With growing confidence and competence, the leadership style can then also reduce its emphasis on relationships.

The emphases on task and relationship are not mutually exclusive. Managers use both forms of leadership, to varying extents, depending on the situation and the particular member of staff. For example, a care assistant in a home for older people may help residents to get up in the morning, sensitively and in a manner which respects their dignity, but her ability to produce a report for a case conference, on a resident for whom she is the keyworker, may be poor. Little would need to be done in respect of the former, apart from occasional reinforcement (relationship) but much would need to be done directly (task) in respect of the latter. For the sake of simplicity, four modes of situational leadership can be identified:

TELLING (HIGH TASK/LOW RELATIONSHIP)
One-way communication. What, when, how etc.
Direction.
SELLING (HIGH TASK/HIGH RELATIONSHIP)
Direction still provided, but two-way communication attempting to get staff member to 'own' the ability/skill.
PARTICIPATING (LOW TASK/HIGH RELATIONSHIP)
Staff member has the knowledge and ability, reinforced through relationship.
DELEGATING (LOW TASK/LOW RELATIONSHIP)
Staff member, high in knowledge and ability. Staff member given authority. (See section on delegation, below.)

The emphasis we have given to the importance of situational factors in shaping leadership styles in relation to task and relationship behaviour should not be interpreted as implying that managers should passively succumb to the situation in which they find themselves. Situational factors can be worked on by the manager so that her access to information, support and resources is increased. For example, a manager may need to build up access to decision-makers in the organization, make alliances with other managers and identify or construct support networks. Such outward-looking leadership will extend influence. For example, in a large organization the manager's chances of placing items on the policy agenda or obtaining expenditure for a new development will be increased if the manager has recognized the importance of working on situational factors.

Dealing with stress

So far, we have suggested ways in which planning can be undertaken, priorities can be decided upon, time can be well used and leadership can be exercised. We are confident that, if our suggestions are carried through, they will help to reduce the strain experienced by social care managers. People can work very hard for quite long periods of time. However the day of reckoning will finally dawn if there is no opportunity for replenishment. Managers often become adept at predicting levels of sick leave amongst staff, based on crisis periods in their establishments, but they are usually far less aware of their own stress points. The point at which pressure becomes stress will vary from individual to individual.

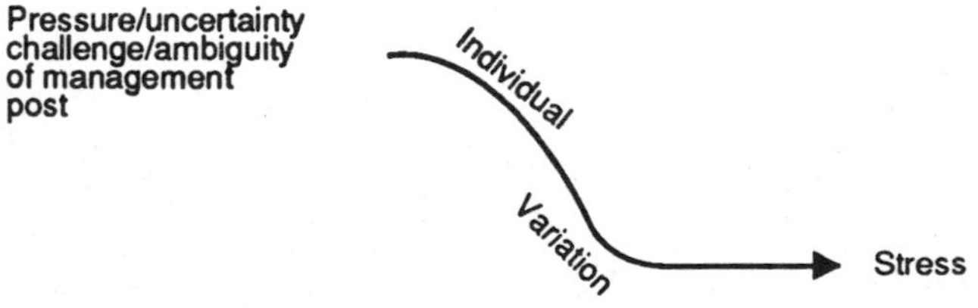

Pressure/uncertainty
challenge/ambiguity
of management
post

Individual

Variation

Stress

Figure 2.2   Transition from pressure to stress.

McDerment (1988) offers the following list of possible reactions to dysfunctional stress experienced by workers in social care settings:

1. High resistance to going to work every day.
2. A sense of failure.
3. Anger and resentment.
4. Guilt and blame.
5. Discouragement and indifference.
6. Negativism.
7. Isolation and withdrawal.
8. Feeling exhausted all day.
9. Frequent clock-watching.
10. Great fatigue after work.
11. Loss of positive feeling towards clients.
12. Postponing client contacts.
13. Stereotyping clients.
14. Inability to concentrate on or listen to what the client is saying.
15. Feeling immobilized.
16. Cynicism regarding clients; a blaming attitude.
17. Increasingly 'going by the book'.
18. Sleep disorders.
19. Avoiding discussions of work with colleagues.
20. Self-preoccupation.
21. More approving of behavioural-control measures such as tran-
    quillizers.
22. Frequent colds and 'flu.
23. Frequent headaches and gastro-intestinal disturbances.
24. Rigidity in thinking and resistance to change.
25. Suspicion and paranoia.
26. Excessive use of drugs.
27. Conflict in personal relationships.
28. High absenteeism.

For the manager, reactions 11 to 14 and 16 can equally apply to her dealings with staff members. We have probably all known managers who, because they were under stress, postponed contact with staff, were unable to concentrate sufficiently on what staff were saying, or only had a residue of negative feelings to those around them.

The manager working under personal stress is likely to do more damage to staff, service users and other managers than someone nursing a heavy cold! She is likely to make snap judgments, to over-simplify issues by dismissing alternatives, to polarize staff, to lose her sense of perspective, and to generate crises from minor incidents. She is also likely to make others stressed!

However it is too simple to assume that some people are more susceptible to stress than others. Stress is an occupational hazard in social care which is likely to affect everyone at some point in some way. It may be helpful to reflect on the characteristics of social care management which may make it stressful:

- the relentless nature of the work,
- the emotional demands of the work,
- the undermining of self-worth from persistent external criticism,
- the exposed position of leadership.

It may be helpful to reflect on the specific pressures in your job.

Activity

Pressures in the job situation

All of us work in situations we may not regard as ideal. Where are the pressures in your job?

A. **Identify one or two major work areas or tasks in which you have recently been engaged:**

   1.
   2.

B. **Place a tick in the appropriate column to indicate how your work was affected by the adequacy of each of the factors below:**

A – ADEQUATE   C – SIGNIFICANTLY INADEQUATE
B – A LITTLE INADEQUATE   D – COMPLETELY INADEQUATE

		A.	B.	C.	D.
1.	Personal Time	—	—	—	—
2.	Resources (Money, Staff, Equipment, Materials)	—	—	—	—
3.	Personal encouragement and support	—	—	—	—
4.	Organizational recognition and status	—	—	—	—
	Reward	—	—	—	—

		A.	B.	C.	D.
5.	Definition of role and contribution	—	—	—	—
6.	Cooperation	—	—	—	—
7.	Authority/Discretion	—	—	—	—
8.	Personal knowledge and skill	—	—	—	—
9.	Information	—	—	—	—
10.	Organizational influence	—	—	—	—

Front-line managers in social care settings are often mediators between two cultures; the culture of practice and the culture of higher managers. A Social Services Inspectorate Report of a study of first line managers in day and domiciliary services (SSI, 1988) referred to this role as that of 'player-manager'. This role as mediator is a source of tension. Difficult or seemingly impossible decisions have to be made in meeting the expectations of higher managers to cope within the constraints of existing resources. Simultaneously, in their contact with staff and clients, social care managers have to call on their powers of concentration, energy and creativity. In other words, social care managers are involved not only in rationing resources but also in rationing, or not rationing, themselves. This is a potentially stressful mix of overload of work and overloaded emotions. Fortunately, the problem of personal stress for those working in the field of social care is becoming recognized and 'burn-out' is the cause of much concern. But how can burn-out be avoided?

Some managers never seem to get round to taking their full holiday entitlement. This is negligence! It is also unwise to fritter the whole of a holiday entitlement away in odd days, because many managers need as much as a week to wind down.

Managers can be beset by change in their daily lives at work and heavy demands in terms of their working relationships. Much of their work can seem fleeting and transient. At the end of the day, or night, there is often a sense of much having been done but an inability to recall it. In such circumstances managers need some form of compensating stability and sense of continuity. For some managers these personal needs will be met almost entirely outside the workplace. For others it is important to establish significant relationships with others at work. Many managers aspire to being the solitary, self-contained coper when it is highly likely that a close relationship with a colleague, from which the manager gains advice and a sense of perspective, will be more helpful in coping with pressure. A sense of perspective can also be gained from other sources: for example, supervision with a higher manager. Managers can also take some measures themselves to reduce personal stress. For some managers this can be as simple as giving themselves recognition for their achievements. Every manager has experienced failure. Managers who dwell on failure could benefit from a personal audit of their credit – their achievements and strengths.

Discussing personal stress can seem self-indulgent. Stress is not the sole prerogative of managers, as is often implied. It can be a problem for any staff. However it is important for managers to remind themselves of the effect their stress can have on others. Conversely, if a manager has a sense of balance, a sense of perspective and proportion, there are important positive consequences. She is more likely to collaborate with colleagues, to develop the ability to delegate and take risks, to be innovative. She is less likely to be striving to impress staff and defensively holding onto the detailed running of the service.

Some pressure, uncertainty and ambiguity will always be part of the world of the manager. Indeed this is part of the challenge of a management post. However the stimulation provided by the demands placed on the manager can all too easily slide over into personal stress. For many social care managers the dividing line between pressure and stress is crossed at the point at which difficult situations shade into the impossible, often because of conflicting expectations on the manager, as with the manager who is simultaneously expected to cut back substantially on her budget *and* make dramatic improvements in service provision! The manager needs a sense of perspective in order to hover above the complexities of working life and thus to maximize her contribution.

Activity

Psychological job description. Increasing demands are being made on social care managers for improved standards of care. Managers' ability to tolerate pressure and ambiguity vary considerably. Similarly, jobs vary in the nature of their demands. Work through your job description and draw out aspects of the job, other than the straightforward duties, which make demands on you. Are there any ways of dealing with these potentially stressful dimensions?

The survival of the manager, and the quality of her performance, depend not just on managing time, managing staff, managing the world outside and all of the other areas covered in this book but also on minimizing personal stress through the recognition of its causes and taking action about it.

Delegation

Delegation, giving to the lowest level possible the authority to carry out work, is a concept to which most managers subscribe. A few managers actually practise it! Managers frequently complain that they have to work harder and harder to stay on top of their jobs. It is useful, therefore, to question whether managers are undertaking work which could be handled by other members of staff. Delegation does not just happen. You will only improve your skills of delegation by analysing your workload, your style of management, your staff. Delegation involves:

GIVING AUTHORITY: giving to a staff member an area of work in which the staff member can take decisions and is given the resources to carry them through in order to achieve results.

SHARING ACCOUNTABILITY: making the staff member answerable for her actions in taking on the AUTHORITY which has been delegated.

We can see, then, that delegation is not *direction*. It is not the same as 'giving out work'. When delegation is practised the staff member decides with the manager on the results to be aimed for, in general terms, and plans how to achieve them, exercising control over the necessary resources. The staff member's performance is monitored at intervals. She has freedom of action and freedom from interference and may do things differently from the manager. The manager's role is to support the staff member, offer suggestions and provide training. In contrast, the manager who 'gives out work' to a staff member specifies the way the work is carried out, monitors it closely and offers little scope for decision-making on the part of the staff member. Delegation is also not *abdication*! Managers need to give help and advice when needed. They need to make sure resources are available, and that results are being achieved. Abdication demoralises staff. They can become uncertain, poorly equipped and inadequately trained.

The type of delegation we have described offers a number of benefits. Firstly, delegation ensures that decisions are taken at the lowest possible level, closer to the relevant information. Secondly, delegation allows more flexible and sensitive practice to develop, because fuller use is made of staff members' potential. Thirdly, delegation frees a manager's time for planning and innovation.

Activity

Try to identify any resistance to delegation which you have by ticking any of the following statements which apply to you:

I don't want to give up my grasp of the detailed running of the service.
I don't want staff members to get the credit/steal the glory.
I still enjoy doing the job from which I was promoted.
I avoid important parts of my job by involving myself in more trivial matters.
I feel that being busy, and being seen to be busy, is more important than achieving results.
My staff haven't the experience and/or training to accept increased responsibility.
I don't want to put myself at risk of something going wrong.

It may be that, if you are resistant to delegation, your resistance is based on an experience of failure. However, on closer examination, it is usually possible to identify reasons for the failure of delegation:

- Staff may have insufficient knowledge, training or experience;
- Staff may not have been given the resources to achieve the desired results;
- Staff may not have been given clearly defined areas of authority;
- The manager's basic approach to delegation may have been faulty. It may have been closer to *direction* or *abdication*.

Planning to delegate: starting-points

One starting-point for improving your approach to delegation is the section on managing time, earlier in the chapter. That section should have helped you to sort out how you apportion your time to your chosen priorities. The other starting-point for improving your skills of delegation is Chapter 7, on managing to train. When you have worked through that chapter, you should have a framework for the identification of the training needs of each staff member which can tell you:

- the knowledge, skills and experience possessed by the staff member; which of these are in use? which could be used or how can they be utilized more fully?
- the areas of work the staff member does well.
- the areas of work the staff member has the potential to undertake, following training.

With this information, part of your supervision of a staff member can include discussion of proposed additional authority, together with the identification of the knowledge and skills required and how these are to be acquired if they are not already present.

Delegation will not produce results overnight and it may give the manager some additional difficulties to work through. Managers are taking chances in practising delegation; although the risks can be minimized, there will be mistakes to be weathered and staff who need to be supported. Developing delegation requires perseverance. Initially, it will be 'quicker to do it yourself' and you may lose some of your command of the detail of the running of the service. Despite these problems, delegation is one of the most powerful means of achieving results in social care management.

Postscript

If you intend to implement any of the suggestions made in this chapter, changing your ways will not be easy! There are three keys to the breaking of old habits and the acquisition of new ones:

1. Launch the new practice as strongly as possible.
2. Never let an exception occur until the new habit is firmly established.
3. Use the first possible opportunity to act on the new practice.

3 Managing others: individual members of staff

How to read this chapter . . .
This chapter is about face-to-face work with individual members of staff. There are sections on selection, correction, disciplinary, grievance and counselling interviews.

After a general introduction, each section follows a broadly similar pattern: preparation, running the interview, after the interview. You will probably find it tedious to work through this chapter from beginning to end. We suggest that you read the introduction and then take it a section or two at a time in any order you please.

Introduction

Much of the work in managing social care involves trying to achieve results through face-to-face discussions with other people; what we might broadly refer to as interviews. Interviewing is used for a number of different purposes, including selecting staff, obtaining information, resolving problems, clearing up misunderstandings, sorting out grievances and so on.

When you use the techniques of interviewing as part of your management role a number of questions may pass through your mind:

- how much talking should the interviewer do?
- what if the interviewee dries up?

- how can an atmosphere which is positive and purposeful be encouraged?

Add to this the pressures to make the right decision, usually quickly, and interviewing looks like a recipe for stress! How can the difficulties be minimized?

Preparation

Whatever the nature of the interview, it is important to spend time in preparing for it and a number of principles can be used to guide such preparation.

Clarify the purpose of the interview.   At the outset it is useful to question whether the interview is necessary. What is its objective? Is a face-to-face interview the best way to accomplish the objective?

Study the subject.   Before any sort of interview it is important to decide on the main issues to be dealt with. Once the main issues are clear, collect together all the necessary information. Ask yourself, where are the difficult areas likely to be?

Outline an interview plan.   All the preparation you have undertaken will be wasted if you do not use the interview systematically. So:

- decide how you will receive the person to be interviewed;
- think about the initial statement you will make;
- be ready with the opening questions;
- have some idea of the desired outcome, but be prepared to modify this as the interview progresses.

Have everything ready.   Allow plenty of time and choose a suitable place for the interview, ensuring that you will be free from interruptions.

Running the interview

When beginning the interview, you should ensure that the *subject is properly introduced*. State the purpose and scope of the interview: for example, is it informal or official, is it confidential? Provide any necessary background information. Then set out the sequence of the interview. *Guide the interview*, according to its purpose. At the end, *give a summary* to establish the results of the interview. Make sure you state any conclusions and that you are clear about what has been agreed and what is left to be resolved. State what action is to be taken. Make any necessary notes.

After the interview

Think back to your preparation for the interview and your interview plan. How did the interview itself compare? If you do not feel satisfied with the way the interview went, ask yourself some questions:

- Was the interview unsuccessful for reasons outside the interview? What were they?
- If not, where did things go wrong?
- What could have been done to improve the interview?

Activity

1. **List the interviews in which you have been involved over the last week or month (maximum 6) and try to state the purpose of each interview.**

   INTERVIEW   PURPOSE

   Select one of these interviews for the remainder of the activity.

2. **Look back at the material on *preparation*. Work through it. How did your preparation measure up?**

                                       YOUR INTERVIEW

   Clarifying the purpose
   Studying the subject
   Outlining a plan
   Being ready

3. **Look back at the material on *running the interview*. How well-run was your interview?**

                                       YOUR INTERVIEW

Introducing the subject
Guiding the interview
Giving a closing summary

4. **Look at the material above on *after the interview*. This activity has, in effect, taken you through a post-interview review of the kind described.**

The stages set out above can be used to think about any interview in which you may be engaged. However there are several different types of interview which deserve to be considered separately, because the *nature* of an interview should fine-tune the structure and style of the interaction. Given the proximity of working relationships in many social care settings, the dynamics are all the more complex. It is all too easy for the one-to-one interview to fall foul on occasion to inappropriate informality: for example, a personal discussion which takes place in a public setting such as a staff room or in front of service users, or which is attempted hurriedly over a break period.

The selection interview

It is difficult to over-estimate the importance of selection interviewing as part of the manager's role. Obtaining the best person available at the required time can be a time-consuming business. The consequences of getting it wrong are far-reaching. It is somewhat salutary to pause and consider the financial implications. Expenditure on staffing usually constitutes the largest proportion of the manager's budget. We need, therefore, to rely on more than just hunches in selecting staff. An approach is needed which assesses each applicant's knowledge, skills and potential for development against the requirements of the job and in the context of the work group within which the successful applicant will have to operate.

Selection interviewing can either contribute to increased effectiveness in the service provided, through the appointment of competent and motivated staff, or, if carried out sloppily, can be part of a vicious spiral of job dissatisfaction, high turnover and a minimum acceptable level of care. It is far easier to appoint an unsuitable or apathetic staff member than it is to dismiss a member of staff who was wrongly selected. The ripples of dismissal can affect the image of a service and other members of staff, and can embroil the manager in trade union and even legal issues. Nevertheless it is not necessary to be an expert on, for example, equal opportunities legislation when someone is appointed or on what constitutes 'fairness' when someone is dismissed. Expert advice can be obtained, if necessary. It is much more important to be committed to the spirit of the legislation. For instance, equal opportunities legislation has the potential to *advance* the recruitment of those applicants such as black people who may have experienced disadvantage, rather than being seen as existing solely to *monitor* the manager's actions.

Preparation

Job description.   At the outset, the objective is to ensure that you have a thorough understanding of the vacancy. Then the job description needs to be prepared or, if you are in a large organization, the Personnel Section may have a standard job description for the particular post, which needs to be checked, and if necessary, updated in respect of your service.

Person profile.   In the recruitment of higher managers great weight is given to specifying not just the job to be filled but also the type of person required. In other areas of selection this is unfortunately often not the case, with the result that the selection process becomes even more subjective than it is already! It is important that you are clear about the knowledge, skills and attitudes you are looking for in the person required for a particular post. In addition, which knowledge, skills and attitudes are essential and which are desirable? Anyone without the essential attributes should not be appointed! Weighing candidates who possess the *essential* attributes against each other according to the *desirable* attributes they also possess may help to clarify who is the best person for the job. In clarifying desirable attributes it is important to be vigilant about the possibility of race and gender bias and to be conscious of the need for affirmative action.

Activity

Think about a particular post for which you are responsible. If you have, or are about to have, a vacancy, think of that post. Write out a person profile:

	ESSENTIAL ATTRIBUTES	DESIRABLE ATTRIBUTES
KNOWLEDGE		
SKILLS		
ATTITUDES		

If you find this difficult, try to think of the attributes of people whom you regard as successful and unsuccessful in this type of job.

Short-listing and interview preparation. Consider the application forms carefully with your person profile to hand. Read for gaps, inconsistencies, ambiguities. Read the references; read between the lines. Any omissions? Work out a plan for the interview. If you are interviewing with a panel, agree the plan *before* the interview starts! Determine the roles of the panel members and the areas each member will explore.

Running the interview

Welcome the applicant. If it is a panel interview, introduce the other panel members and explain who they are and why they are there. Check that the applicant received information about the vacancy and any other information which was sent. Explain the plan of the interview. If the applicant has issues which need to be clarified as a result of this information, deal with them at this stage. Remember that your task is to get the best out of the interviewee in order to help make the selection process easier. Consider the interview as a two-way process which is about negotiation rather than confrontation.

At the end of the interview, explain when the decision will be made and how applicants will be notified. Don't forget interview expenses!

Activity

If you have already undertaken selection interviewing, write down your personal dos and don'ts for interviewers. If you do not have experience of interviewing, use your personal experience of being interviewed to reflect on dos and don'ts! Here are a few examples to start you off.

DOS	DON'TS
Be non-threatening	Ask yes/no questions
Use open-ended questions	Ask leading questions
Use follow-up questions	Interrogate!

**Allow the applicant to add any
additional information as well as
the opportunity to ask questions**

After the interview

If you have drawn up a person profile beforehand you will be able
to compare each candidate against it, either by having taken notes
on each of the applicants in relation to each of the headings on
your profile or by simple scoring, say on an A–D scale under each
of the headings. This should provide plenty of material to assist the
decision on which candidate to select. How will candidates be
informed of the outcome?

After all this effort has been put into the selection of a member
of staff, the lack of induction training or supervision can still wreck
the appointment!

The correction interview

The correction interview should not be confused with the disciplinary interview. Its purpose is to try to *avoid* the need to take
disciplinary action against a member of staff. This type of interview
is one of the unpleasant tasks a manager has to face. Undertaking
such an interview may cut across social relationships with staff and
pose stark choices about the rights of staff versus the rights of
clients. These interviews are often charged with emotion and yet
the manager must remain calm. It is counter-productive for the
manager to become a participant in a heated argument. The manager is aiming for a realistic statement on what may well be dis-
agreeable matters to the staff member involved. The manager is
not setting out to make moral judgments or to inflict punishment.
The manager is seeking to improve the situation and to avoid a
recurrence of the problem.

Preparation

It is important to consider the possible consequences of mis-handling the correction interview: a staff member with a permanent
grudge against you, or with a vendetta against the staff group or

certain clients. You should prepare thoroughly in order to minimize the possibility of such consequences. You should include in your preparation a consideration of the staff member's previous record and should note whether the situation is a first occurrence or the most recent recurrence in a long run of poor performance. Does it appear to arise from a lack of knowledge or motivation?

Running the interview

Consider whether you need to have another senior member of staff with you and be sure to record what was said by the member of staff and yourself, together with what action was taken and how the interview ended. The interview should begin by pointing out the difficulty as you see it and highlighting the effects of what has happened. Try to establish agreement about exactly what took place. Give the staff member a chance to reply fully. Be clear about what is expected from the staff member in future and show confidence in the ability of the staff member to improve.

After the interview

Check that there is no recurrence and do *not* be antagonistic towards the member of staff. If the problem recurs, does it warrant disciplinary action? If it does not recur, try to give the staff member positive recognition for the improvement.

Activity

Reflect on your work as a manager. Is there a correction situation you have been seeking to avoid? If you can bring an example to mind, try to identify why you have avoided it and work through the material on *preparation* again, applying it to the situation you have been trying to avoid.

The disciplinary interview

The disciplinary interview can be the most difficult aspect of the manager's job. It may rupture social relationships which have been built up over many years. The build-up to disciplinary interviews and their aftermath are charged with powerful feelings that are likely to reflect quite different views about management action. Yet the manager must seek to contain the matter to the issues at stake in order to improve the performance of the staff member, or remove her, and to protect clients from any diminution in their quality of life or their exposure to unwarranted risks. Disciplinary action is most commonly taken in response to specific actions on the part of a member of staff. These instances are relatively straight-forward compared to situations in which the manager, as a last resort, is using disciplinary action to rectify generally poor perform-ance which lacks a glaring act of omission or commission on the part of the staff member.

Preparation

You need to familiarize yourself with all of the circumstances, collecting statements from witnesses and having to hand information concerning the staff member's previous work history. You need to know your case and your staff member. You will also need to be clear about your organization's approach to disciplinary action:

- What is the problem? What is the staff member doing, or not doing, which is adversely affecting her work? What are the consequences?
- Is there a disciplinary procedure? If there is, have you followed it?
- Is there a precedent for the way this type of case has been handled?
- Are there any legal implications?
- Have you informed the staff member of her right to be rep-resented by a trade union official or an officer of a professional association or simply to have a friend present?
- Do you understand the conditions of service?

Running the interview

Your role may be to present the case, to cross-examine the staff member and to be cross-examined by the staff member or her representative, with a senior manager in the chair. Alternatively, you may have to chair the proceedings yourself. If you have to do so, come straight to the point. Try to get some agreement about the facts. Give the member of staff the opportunity to reply fully, and if possible, try to ensure that the member of staff understands the consequences of what she has done. Adjourn to reach a decision and communicate the decision as soon as possible. Indicate how the staff member can improve if this is appropriate and express confidence in her ability to do so. The most obvious pitfalls are:

- poor questioning, for example, failure to probe or the use of leading questions;
- use of the wrong style, for example, angry or argumentative or, conversely, too informal;
- mis-handling digressions;
- having rigid ideas about the outcome;
- mis-handling a member of staff who breaks down;
- failure to keep adequate records.

After the interview

As soon as possible after the interview set out in writing the action to be taken, explain the appeals procedure, if any, and confirm the date at which the matter will be reviewed. Try not to show any antagonism in future dealings with the staff member. Check on progress. If the problem still exists, take further disciplinary action. If the staff member improves, recognize the improvement.

The grievance interview

Managers can be tempted to fight shy of grievances. It is tempting for any of us to become defensive and instinctively deny any criticism voiced by a member of staff. However it is more useful to treat a grievance as a signal that something is going wrong. If something is going wrong, here is an opportunity to put things right. Alternatively, if a manager regards a grievance as unjustified, she can use the opportunity to set the record straight. Two points should be noted at the outset. First, always bear in mind that the apparent grievance may not be the real problem. Secondly, counter-criticism is almost always counter-productive, however unjustified you consider the grievance to be.

Preparation

If possible, take time to investigate beforehand. Be sure of your own rights and powers and the organization's policy on the matter. Check out the organization's grievance procedure.

Running the interview

Welcome the grievance and listen carefully. Restate it and check that you have understood it. Give your own view, and if you have already taken some action state what it is. State any intentions you may have for taking further action and try to end on an appreciative note. It is worth noting that in some situations the grievance will remain unresolved, or may appear unresolved, for the staff member concerned. In such instances it may be appropriate to consider the involvement of a more senior manager.

After the interview

Check that the matter has been satisfactorily resolved and that no substitute grievance has arisen.

The counselling interview

There may be times when supervision sessions shade over into counselling a member of staff about problems she is experiencing. At other times there will need to be an interview with the sole purpose of counselling a member of staff who is beset by problems. This type of interview needs to be approached carefully. It will only work if the manager has the trust of the staff member. The manager cannot rely on status to carry off this type of interview. If there are doubts on this point, you should consider either delegating the interview or pushing it up to a more senior manager for the purpose of ensuring that the interview is conducted by someone in whom the staff member has confidence. Remember that the aim of this interview is to help staff members to solve problems which are impinging on their work life. It is not an opportunity to indulge in psychotherapy!

Preparation

Privacy is clearly essential for this sort of interview. You need to set aside plenty of time to avoid the risk of having to break off at a crucial point. If you have some idea about the nature of the problem, consider whether other people may be able to help. If leave of absence may be necessary, think of how the work could be done in such a way as to minimize the staff member's guilt about taking time off.

Running the interview

A counselling interview should not be regarded as an interview without any structure. Welcome the member of staff and, as far as possible, put her at her ease. Encourage the staff member to state her problem(s) and listen sympathetically. Then try to restate each problem to show that you have understood, and take each one separately. If you think someone else could help, share any information you have. Help the person to decide on a plan of action, if possible. This may be too much to expect and may have to wait until another time. Before closing, emphasize that the interview was confidential and be sure it stays that way. Arrange a follow-up interview.

After the interview

Ensure that you hold a follow-up interview, even if the problems have been resolved and you only spend five minutes checking that that is the case. Use the follow-up interview to bring yourself up to date with any developments. Ensure that any promises that you made at the first interview have been kept.

This chapter has advocated a simple framework for use in a diverse range of interviews which managers undertake in their face-to-face work with individual staff members. The next chapter considers the manager's role in working with staff in groups.

4 Managing others: staff in groups

How to read this chapter . . .
This chapter is about staff meetings and teamwork. The section on staff meetings follows a similar pattern to Chapter 3: after a general introduction about staff meetings, there are sections on Preparation, Running Staff Meetings and After the Meeting.
The section on teamwork is a more general discussion. The chapter lends itself to being read either in one go or as two separate sections.

Introduction

There seems to be a growing attachment to the importance of staff meetings. Before we consider the manager's role in relation to staff meetings, perhaps we should ask, why have a meeting? It is easy to fall into the trap of thinking that the response to almost any issue should be to call a staff meeting. A great many issues can be resolved by a quick consultation with a single member of staff or a longer discussion in supervison. Sometimes two minutes spent with four people separately might be more productive than allocating ten minutes on a staff meeting agenda.

Activity

Write down an issue which you think could be dealt with appropriately in a staff meeting and an issue which could not. Make brief notes about why this is.

There is a wide range of possible responses to this activity. In general terms, the factors which might indicate inclusion of an item on a staff meeting agenda are:

- You wish staff to have information presented to them simultaneously in a common form.
- You wish to obtain immediate responses from staff members as a group.
- You wish to encourage involvement in decision-making.
- You wish staff members to have the opportunity to swap ideas, as this may help resolve an issue or improve the thinking behind a proposed initiative.

Thus staff meetings can have a number of purposes:

- giving and receiving information;
- generating ideas/suggestions;
- solving specific problems;
- making decisions.

Frequently, a staff meeting will combine a number of these purposes. It is important to recognize that staff meetings can fulfil other functions for a group of staff, which are concerned with group processes rather than the content of the agenda. Firstly, there is a sense in which meetings affirm the collective identity of the staff group. At its most basic, the staff meeting defines who belongs to the group and who is valued. Staff members can look around and sense their collective identity. Secondly, the staff group can band together. The staff meeting is the place where the whole group can create a pool of knowledge, experience and history: its own culture. An example of this is the way in which a staff group can quickly understand the nuances and implications of a brief item, in a way which is incomprehensible to an outsider. Thirdly, the points we have mentioned can combine to produce greater commitment by staff members to the decisions made and the objectives to be pursued. Fourthly, in some social care settings, shift work and group living may mean that the staff meeting is the only place where the total staff group comes together. It may also be the only time when the manager is perceived as the leader of the staff team, rather than as the manager to whom individuals relate.

In deciding on the advisability of holding staff meetings, it is important for the manager to take into account these functions of staff meetings and to weigh them against the more formal purposes of meetings. Thus the threshold for holding staff meetings in a large residential establishment might be much lower than in a small day care unit in which all of the staff see each other every day.

There is no guarantee that a staff meeting will achieve its purposes or fulfil its functions. Decisions can be pushed down to the lowest common denominator. They can reflect compromise between conflicting views rather than creativity or innovation. Staff meetings can waste the time of people who are not fully involved in the items discussed and meetings can be swayed by the most articulate, even though their ideas may not be any better than those of other members of staff.

Our view is that staff meetings are worth the effort they involve for the manager, but we would stress the need to use them fully in order to avoid them becoming an irritant or a barrier to the achievement of goals. Staff meetings can be improved through awareness of some of the pitfalls to be avoided, but it is worth pausing at the outset to consider the size and type of meeting with which you are dealing as a manager. The size and hierarchical nature of many social care settings can create some ambiguity about the type of meeting in which staff are engaged. In fieldwork teams of around a dozen it is possible for all of the team members to speak on a more or less equal basis. In residential and day care establishments with 40 or 50 staff, with wide variations in formal status, this will not be possible and the sheer size of the group will be intimidating. Similarly, many Home Care Organizers will face problems in running large meetings for home helps who rarely meet each other. These examples illustrate the attention which needs to be given to the handling of questions and comments and the structuring of participation. Apart from size, other factors may affect the nature of a staff meeting. The frequency of meetings may affect the degree of unity in the staff group. The diversity in the composition of the staff group may mean that some staff are virtually strangers to others, only united by their presence in the meeting and their commitment to the staff group.

Ways to better meetings

Preparation

We have tried to show that there are only certain purposes and
functions that a staff meeting can perform. We now want to sharpen
that focus by suggesting that, when you are planning your staff
meeting, every item you discuss can be placed in one or more of
four categories:

Digesting information. We have emphasized *digesting* information
because, strictly speaking, information of a purely factual nature
could be dealt with in other ways, for example through display on
a notice board. However, if the information needs clarification and
comment in order to make sense of it, or if it has important
implications for staff members, then it may need time for it to be
digested. An example might be a progress report on some change
in practice, like the introduction of attached workers in a residential
establishment.

Generating ideas. Some items may require consideration of areas
of work which need to be devised or developed, as with, for example, a new procedure for handling admissions to a day care unit.
Staff members may be asked to contribute their knowledge, experience, judgement and ideas.

Taking decisions and implementing them. After items involving
decision-making, the allocation of responsibility for carrying out
decisions should be made clear. This allocation of responsibility
could obviously be made outside a meeting, but there are advan-
tages to its inclusion in staff meetings because it enables the staff
group to explore the best way of implementing the decision. It
encourages the staff group to 'own' and carry through the decision
and it enables staff members to understand and influence the way
in which their contribution fits into the decision which has been
made.

Changing the framework. Above and around digesting information, the generating of ideas and decision-making, there is a
framework of rules, routines and procedures within and through

which all the deliberations and activity take place. If, as a manager, you are changing this framework in a fundamental way by introducing policies and procedures which constitute a new framework, staff members may feel threatened. It is important to deal with dissent openly in a staff meeting. It is dangerous to close a discussion and make a dictatorial decision. You cannot expect quick decisions if you are changing a framework which includes routines previously central to staff's working lives. This may require the manager to spread such discussion and decision-making over a period of time (see Chapter 8).

Activity

Look back at your last staff meeting. List the items on the agenda. Allocate each item to one or more of the categories discussed above by placing ticks in the columns:

ITEM	DIGESTING INFORMATION	GENERATING IDEAS	TAKING DECISIONS	CHANGING THE FRAMEWORK
1.				
2.				
3.				
4.				

Was there a preponderance of items in a particular category? Does analysing the meeting in this way help to make sense of its process?

   This activity may be a useful starting-point in preparing for a future meeting. It could help you to clarify what you expect from each of the items for that meeting and help you to sort out the kinds of contributions you want to encourage.

Running the meeting

The agenda.   The agenda should not be scribbled down 5 minutes before the meeting starts! Many managers find it useful to solicit items for the agenda from staff members, well before the meeting is due to take place. A good agenda can speed up a meeting. The main point in drawing up the agenda is not to be vague. For example, 'Admissions' does not tell staff very much about what to expect, whereas 'reconsideration of the establishment's procedures on preparation for admission, particularly pre-visits and pre-admission contact between potential residents and existing residents' helps staff to form some views in advance. An agenda which looks long as a result of this sort of planning is to be welcomed. A long agenda that is the result of putting in too many items for the time available for the meeting is to be avoided! Perhaps you wish to draw on the last activity and give pointers to staff alongside each item: for example, 'For information', 'For discussion', 'For decision'. Obviously items which need urgent decisions have to come before those that can wait. Other aspects are less obvious. The beginning of a meeting tends to be livelier than the end, so if you want lots of ideas the item concerned needs to feature early on. You can predict that some items will unite the staff group and others will divide it. Making conscious choices with respect to this factor can affect the staff's reaction to the whole meeting. If possible, find a unifying item to end the meeting. A problem which often emerges is spending too long on trivial, urgent items, to the exclusion of important issues. This can be avoided by putting timings on each agenda item. Finally, aim not just to *start* promptly but also to *finish* promptly. Set a maximum length for the meeting. We suggest one and a half hours.

Activity

Measure your last staff meeting agenda against the above discussion. Are there any things you would like to amend at the next meeting?

Chairing.   Clearly one of the important issues in staff meetings is achieving an effective level of structure and control: something between anarchy and dictatorship! The chairing of the meeting is crucial. Taking the chair at a staff meeting affects people in different ways. Some managers relish the imposition of their will on the meeting. Berating the staff is the order of the day, interspersed with rituals of acquiescence extracted from the staff. Other managers feel that getting staff together 'to have their say' is an end in itself and have staff meetings which seem to achieve very little. Staff meetings then become an excuse for indecision. In either of these cases, such self-gratification on the part of managers is a barrier to the effectiveness of a staff meeting.

An indication of self-gratification is talking a lot from the chair. Chairing is essentially a process of enabling others to talk and ensuring that they experience the meeting as having achieved its goals. For meetings to be regarded as useful, rather than pleasant, by the staff group they have got to get somewhere – somewhere the individual staff member could not have reached on her own. To chair is to serve; it is to assist the staff group towards the best discussion and decision-making: it involves interpretation, clarification and the ability to move the discussion forward. The manager must possess a commitment to the collective objectives of the meeting which staff can readily perceive. A sense of purpose concerning the need to reach the best solution as quickly as possible is more important than a charismatic personality. Structure and control then become an issue of completing the business, rather than pulling rank.

Structuring the discussion   It may seem odd to talk about structuring a discussion – isn't the idea of staff meetings to get staff speaking freely? Yes and no. Staff meetings involve discussion with a purpose. We cannot offer a single script for running a discussion, but we can suggest some questions which may help when discussion is bogged down:

Why is this item on the agenda?
Can we establish a shared view?
What is our shared view?
Why do we hold it?
Can we agree on a way forward?

As far as the final point is concerned, it is often best taken in two stages. The manager can set out a series of options and avoid being dismissive, and then work through each of them as a precursor to the final decision. On complicated items she might want to draw the staff's attention to this process by using flip chart paper to write down and make notes on the above questions.

Closing the discussion.   You may not always be able to reach a conclusion on an item. An item may be better left unresolved because:

- more information is required;
- views are needed from people who are not present;
- more time is needed to think issues through;
- events may change soon;
- there is not enough time to do an item justice;
- two or three staff members can satisfactorily deal with items outside the staff meeting.

However avoid using these legitimate reasons for leaving items unresolved as a rationalization for avoiding a difficult decision or avoiding a confrontation over an unpopular decision. At the end of each item, the chairperson should briefly summarise what has been agreed. This is not just a question of keeping the record straight but also of conveying a sense of achievement. The chairperson should also indicate who is taking any follow-up action.

Dealing with the process. Give some thought to the seating arrangements you want in order to facilitate the meeting. For example, having staff members in rows facing you will not facilitate sharing in decision-making! There are three measures you can take to help a staff meeting's process.

Firstly, do not come down like a ton of bricks when suggestions are made. Having staff members in fear of hostility or ridicule is the surest formula for sterile meetings. Encourage suggestions and get the meeting to work on them. Secondly, when seeking opinions come to senior staff last. If a senior staff member has held forth, other staff may either be inhibited or oppose the senior staff member on principle. Thirdly, close on a note of achievement or unity. If this is not possible, refer to an earlier item on the agenda which was resolved on a positive note.

After the meeting: producing the minutes

It is difficult to chair and to take minutes, so it is hoped that someone else will have taken on this task. But the minutes are still your responsibility. They can be brief, but make sure they include;

Date of the meeting.
All agenda items.
List of attenders.

Decisions reached and main arguments.
Name of person responsible for any action.
Date and time of next meeting.

In stressing the mechanisms which help to produce efficient staff meetings we would not wish to lose sight of the issue of effectiveness. You can set up regular staff meetings which have all the administrative details well executed, which begin and end on time and which you chair admirably – but which produce nothing of any use. Effectiveness can only be measured by the extent to which a staff meeting achieved its objectives. If decisions were on the agenda, were they made? If information was to be digested was it understood?

Activity

Write down up to three changes you think are necessary in your staff meetings which could be implemented immediately.

Teamwork

We turn now to teamwork. As a manager, one of your roles with staff is that of team leader. Teamwork is an important component in modifying and developing services, part of a continuing developing response to changing needs. Within the social care context the issue of teamwork is complex, because of the degree of personal involvement in the work and also because 'a team' can refer to a group of staff, often large in number, which, owing to shift patterns and work practices, may not work together as a unit, or whose members may not even work with the same colleagues from one shift to another. Given such features of social care settings, in what sense are staff groups 'teams'? This is an important question, because a continual striving for an elusive sense of teamwork can sap rather than build up morale. Payne and Scott (1982) draw together material on this point and highlight the distinction between teams and networks. In a team, staff are engaged in frequent face-to-face work, often with the whole group working together. By contrast, in a network, people come together to undertake particular tasks and individuals come and go throughout a working cycle. Payne and Scott illustrate the distinction between teams and networks by the use of a sporting analogy. Thus a football team is quite clearly a 'team'. An athletics team is a network. It is important therefore that a manager has an understanding of the stages in team development and is able to recognize the stage her 'team' has reached.

More general approaches to group processes are relevant to an understanding of teamwork. (See Brown 1986, Ch. 4). For example, Tuchmann (1965) suggests that groups typically form, storm and norm before they perform:

FORMING	There is anxiety, dependence on the leader, testing to find out the nature of the situation and what behaviour is acceptable.	Members find out what the task is, what the rules are, what methods are appropriate.
STORMING	Conflict between subgroups, rebellion against leader, opinions polarized, resistance of control by groups.	Emotional resistance to the demands of the task.
NORMING	Development of group cohesion, resistance overcome and conflicts patched up, mutual support and development of group feeling.	Open exchange of views and feelings. Cooperation develops.
PERFORMING	Interpersonal problems are resolved; roles are flexible and functional.	Emergence of solutions to problems. Constructive attempts at task completion. Energy is now available for effective work.

Such stages in group development are not necessarily sequential. They may slip a stage, or double back or all flash by in one meeting. Again, different levels in an organization may be at different stages. For example, a large children's home may be located in a Social Services Department in the throes of reorganization which is generating a good deal of storming, the whole staff team in the children's home may be norming and a staff team in a particular unit may be performing.

There is a considerable amount of literature specifically on developing teamwork. For the purpose of this discussion, attention is focused on four main stages of team development (after Woodcock, 1979) which are:

1. The *undeveloped* team.
2. The *experimenting* team.
3. The *consolidating* team.
4. The *mature* team.

As teams develop certain characteristics emerge and the processes within the group begin to change. Teams which seek to improve their effectiveness tend to pass through a number of developmental stages during which certain characteristics can be observed. Attempts to categorize these stages and the signs they exhibit are inevitably an over-simplification. For example, a team that is well-developed may have periods when it appears to be losing all cohesion, although it may be achieving its objective. However a model based on the four stages is helpful in enabling teams to recognize where they are, or want to be, in the developmental process. It is unlikely that a team will display all the characteristics of a particular phase, so it will usually be a grouping of prominent features which indicates where a team stands in terms of its development.

The undeveloped team

- The most common 'team' in which individuals come together for a special purpose but have not spent time considering how to work together.
- No attempts are made to discuss feelings openly.
- Feelings are seen as something for private life and not for the workplace.
- Team members conform to an established line in which procedures dictate outcomes. Even constructive ideas may not be welcomed.
- Meetings tend to consist of a series of statements with members expressing their own views, more talking than listening, and rarely challenging leadership.
- Decision-making is the domain of the leader, others confining themselves strictly to their own defined jobs.
- In short, no real teamwork.

Progression from the 'undeveloped' stage to the 'experimenting' stage is likely to be the major step in team development because it becomes clear that a decision has been taken to try to improve the team's functioning.

The experimenting team

- A rigorous review of operating methods is undertaken with a view to improved performance.
- Problems are faced and underlying values and beliefs debated.
- Temporary feelings of insecurity, which result from consideration of controversial issues, are experienced.
- A genuine concern for the views of colleagues may bring increased listening as well as allow personal animosities to surface and be confronted.
- The team may become introspective and be dynamic at the same time, and so be uncomfortable to be in.

Despite becoming more open and with a greater potential to be effective, it is likely that the team will still lack the ability to work in a unified and methodical way. The learning gained from addressing interpersonal issues needs to be put to profitable use.

The consolidating team

- Here we see the beginnings of confidence and trust which enables operating methods to be closely examined.
- A more systematic approach tends to be adopted, leading to a clearer and methodical style of working.
- Rules and procedures may be reintroduced to form agreed guidelines with greater group commitment.
- Relationships improve.
- Planning and reviewing become more evident.

Working through this stage and building on the interpersonal experiences of the 'experimenting' period will form the basis for the development of a mature team. The team has begun to integrate the elements of relationships, methods and ground rules in effective ways.

The mature team

- Flexibility is the keynote, with different procedures for different needs.
- Leadership becomes more democratic, with full team involvement in decision-making.
- Individual commitment to the team's success is paramount, with a balance of team pride and individual initiative.
- The contribution of the team to the wider organizational structures becomes apparent.
- Development becomes an increasing priority.

Above all the team will be experienced as positive and rewarding for all team members.

For managers it is worth remembering that teams rarely work by chance. Effective team-bulding is each member's responsibility and will take time to develop.

Activity

The following questions can be used to guide your reflection on your team's performance and should help you to decide the stage the team has reached.

1. Do you know what team you are in and who is in it?
2. Does your team meet regularly?
3. Does the team have a clear idea of its mandate?
4. Does the team have a method of evaluating its work?
5. Does your team have a high turnover of members?
6. Does the team discuss issues together?
7. Are the decision-making processes in your team overt or covert?
8. Do you find support within your team or do you have to seek it outside the team?
9. Can you share feelings honestly in team meetings – or can feelings only be expressed indirectly in games and manipulation?
10. How does the team deal with conflict?
11. Is it safe to reveal your mistakes in your team?
12. How successful is your team at solving its own problems?

                                        (Woodcock, 1979)

The responsibility for team development is an important part of a social care manager's role. In many settings teams are large and the work activities of groups of staff are diverse. An understanding of team development and the ways in which it affects team functioning is thus essential. Woodcock (1979) offers a series of exercises which enable managers to identify team needs, to plan action to improve team development and to review team progress. A useful starting-point is to gain an understanding of team members' views of the stage of development the team has reached, and the following activity, which is adapted from Woodcock, is offered as a basis from which to work:

Activity

The Rating Sheet can be used with all team members (and also with relevant outsiders) to gain understanding of a team's functioning. The sheet is distributed and participants are asked to consider the main characteristics of the four principal stages of development (as outlined previously) and to mark the rating scale according to where they consider the team to be.

RATING SHEET   OUR TEAM AND ITS STAGE OF DEVELOPEMENT

Stage 1	Stage 2	Stage 3	Stage 4
Characteristics of the undeveloped team	Characteristics of the experimenting team	Characteristics of the consolidating team Stage 2 With a more systematic approach.	Characteristics of the mature team Stages 2 and 3 characteristics plus:
1. Feelings not dealt with. 2. The workplace is for work only. 3. Established line prevails. 4. No 'rocking the boat'. 5. Poor listening. 6. Weakness covered up. 7. Unclear objectives. 8. Low involvement in planning. 9. Bureaucracy. 10. Boss takes most decisions.	1. Experimentation. 2. Risky issues debated, wider options debated. 3. Personal feelings raised. 4. More inward-looking. 5. Greater listening. 6. More concern for others. 7. Sometimes uncomfortable.	1. Methodical working. 2. Agreed procedures. 3. Established ground rules.	1. High flexibility. 2. Appropriate leadership. 3. Maximum use of energy and ability. 4. Basic principles considered, agreed and reviewed. 5. Needs of all members met. 6. Development a priority.

The activity will provide information on individuals' analyses of a team's stage of development which can be followed up in supervision sessions. It also enables a group to have access to different perceptions and this can form the basis for discussion to try to achieve consensus on the stage of development. From this it should be possible to formulate an agreed statement about the group. The activity can be used several times throughout a planned programme of development to check progress and reassess needs.

In some teams, the previous activity may be too abstract a starting-point. An alternative approach can be adopted (after Harris and Valentine 1982).

Activity: team study day

Preparation work. **Everyone gives some thought to, and makes notes on, the following:**

- **Individual hopes or fears, likes or dislikes about work.**
- **Individual views of what the team should or should not be doing, both at the level of overall strategy and at the level of any small-scale changes which are thought necessary.**
- **Team members' needs for support and how they might be met.**

The structure and process of the day. The amount of structure employed on the day is obviously important. In simple terms, team members will want to focus on the things which are important to the team, in what seems to be the right sequence and in a constructive frame of mind. It is important to create and maintain the right atmosphere in which to work together in order to make 'progress'.

One of the attractive features of the structure of a study day is that it can preserve a sense of individual identity while at the same time dealing with group identity and working at collective responses the team might develop. It can be experienced as something different, partly because time is set aside for reflection and discussion away from everyday pressures.

On the day itself there needs to be a 'warm-up' before the main work of the day begins. This serves as a transition from the routine of being a busy team member to that of a participant in a study day. This needs to be a stage of group activity which is stimulating but not threatening and which allows people to get involved in a 'safe' way.

Identifying the issues which will form the agenda for the team's development. Randomly selected pairs can be used to develop personal statements based on the preparation work. For 15 minutes each team member shares with her partner, her responses to the preparation work. Her partner encourages expansion of points, elicits feelings etc. The partners then swap roles for a further 15 minutes. Trust and support is encouraged at this stage and later, when each partner presents the other's views at a feedback session. The pairs exercise also demonstrates vividly the importance of shared responsibility, in this case in the task of finding out and representing another person's views to the team. During the feedback everyone has an equal share of the team's attention and this enables each team member's opinion to be registered.

Assembling the issues in priority order. Group identity is the focus of this stage. It focuses attention on the strength of the team and its ability to operate collectively. For many teams in which members have worked fairly independently the extent to which people feel identified with their team is often uncertain and this uncertainty may be an obstacle to effective teamwork. In so far as a team's identity arises from the pooling of the characteristics of each individual, as well as the functions a team is expected to perform, the presentation of each individual statement can go a long way towards strengthening a team's identity. This can occur when a level of agreement about some issues is unexpectedly discovered, or when shifts of opinion are noted. Perhaps the most significant aspect at this stage is that, when the individual statements are collated, they form a comprehensive list of issues for the team to prioritize. Achieving results will often be seen in terms of agreed statements of intent or team decisions, so agreement about how to progress towards these is required at this stage. From the collated list of items and issues identified by individuals the team has to select those it wishes to work on during the day. If the team is deadlocked and unable to reach decisions by consensus, the single transferable vote can be used. It is useful for the team to consider the way it functions at this stage and to learn from the process used to reach agreement.

Working on the priority issues. Small groups (five to seven people) can work on the selected items, either as special interest groups with particular tasks or as representative groups working on the same task. The purpose is to explore the subject matter and share views in an atmosphere of openness, honesty and trust in order to produce recommendations to put to the whole team at the next stage.

Statements of intent and decision-making. The culmination of the day's work is to reach agreed goals which may or may not have been modified during the day. Achieving the desired results usually takes the form of agreeing plans for the way the team will function or for the way the team will deal with particular issues. It may also include a general feeling that an item or problem has had a fair hearing and people want to leave with some optimism that a debate leading to action can be continued constructively back at work.

The feedback from work in the small groups provides a basis from which a team can progress towards a collective response to the selected items. Whether reaching decisions or exploring possi- bilities, it is useful for the team to consider and learn from its methods of working at this stage. The method of small groups bringing informed agenda items to the full team for a decision is in itself a model. A team could set up a staff meeting as the final activity of the day. Such a team meeting can serve the dual purpose of reaching decisions, whether tentative or binding, and providing a learning instrument by which aspects of the team's meetings can be analysed and modified.

However agreements or decisions are made the general principle we would promote is that, although reaching consensus may be desirable, account must be taken of different interests. It may be important to look at the consequences for individuals of any decisions taken with which they disagree, so that people go away knowing they have been considered. Having emphasized the sig- nificance of everybody's contribution to the pool of ideas and suggestions, it follows that there will be a good deal of business with which the team did not deal. Whatever unfinished business there is, it should be a function of the final stage to plan how this is to be dealt with in the future. This can be experienced as satisfac- tory to those in the minority and further demonstrates the recog- nition of individuals within the team. It goes without saying that achieving results at this stage not only justifies the time spent but for some will determine the success of the day. For most team members the extent to which results are achieved will affect their ability to learn from the day's activities.

5 Managing resources

How to read this chapter . . .
Dull chores or an important component of care? This chapter
explores the management of the internal resources of domestic work
and the building and is intended primarily for managers in residential
and day care establishments. Given the range of social care settings
and the variation in the systems and procedures operating in relation
to the management of resources, the chapter is pitched at a general
level. You can read it as two separate sections or as a whole chapter.

Domestic management

An important aspect of a manager's role is what might be termed
domestic management. Domestic management forms the basis for
the practice of social care in residential and day care settings. This
domestic element, centred around the ordering, preparation and
provision of food and ensuring a safe, healthy living and working
environment, can seem either mundane or all-consuming, sometimes both! Some managers settle for this – the job stops at hotel
management! Many managers' responses to this aspect of management seem to be polarized into two extremes: it is either the be-
all and end-all of their work, or else it is seen as an inconvenience
that gets in the way of 'real' social care management.

A prerequisite of social care management is to ensure that the
practicalities of domestic management are carried out. There must

be efficient systems for the provision of food, heat and light, cleanliness, repairs and maintenance, in order for the establishment to function at an adequate level. If an establishment has developed quick and appropriate responses to needs which are met by domestic management, clients will feel cared for and staff will feel supported. Unresponsive domestic management can lead to frustration and hostility directed at managers which may aggravate relationships and jeopardize other areas of work. A great deal of energy and time can be spent in trying to sort out practical problems or in dealing with inefficiencies: energy and time which could otherwise be spent on service users.

In the area of domestic management a balance has to be found. It is important in its own right, but it is also important to get it right so that it does not swamp a manager's other priorities. What are the issues to consider in striking this balance?

- Are there clear procedures for carrying out the manager's budgetary responsibilities for the staff and the building?
- How much control does the manager have over budgetary responsibilities?
- Who is responsible for repairs and maintenance? Are the procedures adequate?
- Who chooses furniture, pictures, plants and decoration?
- Is there a meaningful choice of food? Is it ethnically appropriate? Is it well presented, served hot and on time?
- Are the surroundings clean and comfortable?
- Is the environment welcoming?
- Is there flexibility in the daily routines?

The issues raised by these questions will undoubtedly affect the atmosphere within an establishment and give rise to expressions of individual taste which may help to counter institutionalizing tendencies which can so easily be depersonalizing for clients. Clearly then, the manager has a role in promoting the importance of domestic management and stressing that it is an integral part of social care. Domestic staff should be regarded as providing a significant dimension in the overall care. In fact, for many establishments, the central importance of food and the social significance of mealtimes is a major contribution to the care of individuals. Kitchen staff may, as a result, assume important roles for clients using the establishment. Similarly domestic staff, by the nature of their work, may be in a position to develop more relaxed relationships with clients, because clients are less likely to be making demands on them. All domestic staff have an important contribution to make to the overall aims of the establishment. Involving domestic staff in regular meetings and in supervision structures may be the most effective way of doing this. Obviously this needs to be balanced by ensuring that the issues discussed are related to the work of domestic staff.

Recognizing the value of the contribution of domestic staff is likely to be encouraged by:

● the availability and relevance of job descriptions;
● effective procedures for staff selection;
● a format for induction and supervision.

The way each of these is utilized will make statements to domestic and other staff. In large residential and day care establishments, it may be appropriate for domestic management to be the main responsibility of one member of the senior staff team. However it must be acknowledged that an over-reliance on supervison provided by one of the senior staff may reinforce feelings of inferiority. For this reason it is important that, in some way, all managers, and especially the manager with overall responsibility for the establishment, are seen to be aware of developments in domestic management.

It is not our intention in any way to suggest that domestic staff are less important than care staff or that the responsibility for managing or supervising domestic staff should be regarded as a marginal area of managerial activity. However, in order to consider in some detail this particular element of the management task in social care settings, it has been necessary to concentrate on domestic management as a separate management function.

Managing the building

This is another area of responsibility for managers in residential and day care establishments which can all too easily be reduced to the status of 'caretaking'. Management of the building, which in some cases will be the home of the clients, will make statements more generally about the care provided by the establishment. A manager needs to set an example for all staff and for users about the treatment of a place which people attend or which is their home. Good decorating and well-maintained facilities are obvious examples of this. Sharing this responsibility with users of the building is important. For example, in a long-stay residential establishment for adults, this may be best achieved by encouraging residents to decorate and furnish their own rooms and by involving residents in making decisions about the use of other rooms and about the decorating and furnishing of them. Managers need to think about the way clients can personalize space in relation to specific establishments. For an adolescent in a residential establishment this may be through putting up posters of pop stars and sports personalities. For an older person it may be by displaying a framed photograph of a relative or a few mementos.

It is important to ensure that the building is used in ways which fulfil the aims of the establishment. This may appear to be stating the obvious. However it is worth reminding ourselves that many of the buildings in use in the residential and day care sectors were erected between 20 and 40 years ago. In the years which have elapsed since their construction many of the buildings have required substantial structural alteration in order to make them suitable for their changing uses. Just as the needs of those requiring care change, so the buildings within which they receive care need to change.

Activity

Think about the establishment you work in. Can you think of changes which have already occurred or which could be made?

Use of:	Changes which have taken place	Changes which could take place
• the building generally;		
• lounges;		
• bedrooms, if any;		
• personalizing space;		
• furniture;		
• decoration.		

The most obvious example is that of buildings which have been structurally altered to provide small group living arrangements out of a previously communally-organized establishment. More recently the introduction of the concept of the resource centre has placed additional pressure on establishments to respond to different service requirements. The effects which these in turn have on the balance of public and private space and the way the establishment is used by those inside and outside the establishment are likely to have a significant impact on the quality of life of clients. There is research evidence which supports the view that control over private space is an essential characteristic of good care (Willcocks *et al.*, 1987).The distinctions between private, public and semi-public space within the establishment are an important determinant of well-being and should not be taken for granted. For managers the ability to recognize different uses of parts of the establishment as well as the ways in which changes should be encouraged is clearly advantageous.

This brief consideration of the management of internal resources in the spheres of both domestic management and the building begins to challenge the assumption that this aspect of social care is unimportant and shows how the manager's role has developed in this area of work. The next chapter will explore the management of external resources.

6 Managing external links

How to read this chapter . . .
   This chapter deals with links external to particular work settings. After a general introduction to the management of such links it considers keyworking, case conferences, working with relatives and volunteers, managing your manager and managing meetings with other managers. Each section can be read separately to follow up specific issues or you can tackle the whole chapter as a means of reviewing external links in a more systematic fashion.

Most social care services are a part of the wider community or have the potential to be. They are in contact with relatives and friends of service users, volunteers, neighbours, shops, pubs, clubs, schools, churches and workplaces. There may be other staff within the agency (managers, personnel and administrative staff for example), voluntary groups, other occupational groups (such as district nurses, health visitors, community psychiatric nurses, general practitioners, consultants, psychologists and the police) – all of whom may shape the nature of external relationships. Developing and maintaining this increasingly elaborate pattern of external links is an important aspect of the manager's role, for a number of reasons. Firstly, these external links can become additional resources to the service for which the social care manager is directly responsible. Secondly, a failure to invest in maintaining links can result in the manager constantly encountering divisiveness, obstruction or non-cooperation. Thirdly, managers can use their external links to provide information about the service for which they are responsible in order to ensure that it is used appropriately.

Managing external links can be fraught with difficulties. Suspicion, hostility and old antagonisms between social care staff and health workers, fieldworkers and others wait to be rekindled. Fieldworkers' assumptions that people are better off in the community; health workers' assumptions that social care managers are too fussy about the delivery of their services; fieldworkers' complaints about poor admission procedures in residential and day care establishments; residential and day care staff's experiences of the 'hit and run' fieldworker – as these examples demonstrate, it is all too easy for miscommunication and distrust to become commonplace.

Most of the impetus for collaboration with people outside the immediate work setting has concentrated on formal committees and joint planning systems. Such attempts at joint work, even if they succeed, may come unstuck in the face of the inability or unwillingness of front-line workers to cooperate.

Activity

Write brief notes about a difficult experience you have had in the management of external links. Now think carefully about the incident:

- **Who said what to whom?**
- **How did each participant behave?**
- **What did you expect of them?**
- **What did they expect of you?**

Write down what you think were the assumptions underlying what was said and done by each participant. Scrutinize your own assumptions. Write down points at which assumptions came into conflict.

The issues raised by this activity are important, as they point to matters which must be attended to if a manager is to make effective use of the contributions of workers and others outside her immediate work setting. The rationale for maintaining or improving external links is clear. Failure to do so may add a further and unnecessary dimension of fragmentation to users' experiences of the service. Divisions between workers can worsen the experience of service users and those close to them.

Activity

Return to your notes made for the previous activity. Shift the focus of your attention away from the assumptions held by workers. Assess the impact that the incident had on the service user concerned and those close to her.

If we are to make effective use of external links three requirements are necessary. Firstly, we must accept the importance of these 'trading relationships' as part of the management role. They must be seen as an important part of a manager's work, which require time and skill, not as a diversion from the 'real work'. Secondly, we must educate ourselves about the working world of our counterparts: their organizations, values, working habits and pressures. Working effectively with the outside world is not a question of simply enforcing our agenda! Opportunities for joint training and joint work can help. Thirdly, we must be wary of seeing collaborative work as being impeded solely by differences in attitudes. Negative stereotyping of other groups with labels which pigeon-hole them into readily recognizable categories is not just an interpersonal problem; it is often a process embedded in the pressures and organizational arrangements of day-to-day work. The structures of service provision often manufacture or reinforce difficulties in collaborative work. For example, in the statutory sector, the post-Seebohm practice of many social services departments of having separate organizational divisions for fieldwork, residential and day care services has left a legacy which has not been easily overcome by subsequent restructuring. Working effectively on external links will be more readily achieved if services are managed at a local level and are accountable to the same manager, and if the local boundaries of other organizations are coterminous with those of social care services. This is rarely the case!

Activity

Write a list of the external links you need to maintain or develop. We suggest that your list be restricted to the six links which you regard as being the most important. In making your list you should reconsider the points made earlier:

- **Will the link generate additional resources?**

- Will failure to develop the link result in your encountering obstruction and non-cooperation?
- Will the link enable you to provide information about your service?

Then write down what you need from each of these external links and what you may need to provide for them.

EXTERNAL LINKS	I NEED FROM THEM	I CAN PROVIDE FOR THEM

As well as having general expectations of what social care managers need from other people and what others need from social care managers, planning to work together in relation to specific service users has to be undertaken.

Keyworking

The concept of the keyworker is well known within social care settings. Different authorities, agencies and work settings have understandably translated these principles into their practice in different ways. This has led to a plethora of titles being used: attached worker, link worker, special worker and so on. One of the strengths of the keyworker concept has been its adaptability to a range of practice settings. Managers need to be conscious of the importance of modifying the concept to their particular setting. Whichever variant of keyworking is adopted it is clear that the principle of having a designated member of staff particularly responsible for the needs of a service user or a small group of service users is accepted as good practice. It enables care to be tailored to the needs of individual clients and it provides a means to enhance jobs by making full use of staff members' potential. Keyworking had probably been the single most influential idea in social care.

A policy statement by SCA and BASW sought to identify features of keyworking. These included:

- Enabling users to meet their full potential, through the use of relationship skills by the keyworker.

- Participation of the user in the process of planning care and selection of the keyworker.
- The need for first line managers to make roles and tasks explicit.

(S.C.A./B.A.SW 1987)

Moving outside the employing agency, the issues raised by the keyworker model are still valid. In particular the concept of the keyworker points to the need for flexibility in jobs, accompanied by clarity about expectations, tasks and responsibilities in order to avoid misunderstandings and consequent gaps in service provision.

Case conferences

Case conferences perform a number of functions. Firstly, and most obviously, they allow those present to pool their knowledge. Secondly, participants can explore alternative courses of action. Thirdly, by sharing out the decision-making, case conferences can be used to reduce the degree of anxiety carried by individual workers. However case conferences also have potentially problematic features. Participants may have different frames of reference; they may have differing degrees of status and power; they may speak different professional languages. Consequently, the chairperson's role is clearly of paramount importance.

Many managers in social care settings are thrust into the role of chairperson. If it is at all possible, we would urge managers to resist this in favour of having an independent chairperson. The social care manager has a contribution to make to a case conference which should not be fettered by having to strive for impartiality. Whoever chairs a case conference, it is an important job with many elements. The chairperson has to take on the task of clarification. This can be as simple as introducing people to each other, but it can become more complicated when elucidating participants' roles or sorting out the circumstances confronted by the conference in relation to policy and legal issues. The chairperson has to walk a tightrope between encouraging contributions and cutting down extraneous material. She may have to arbitrate if conflict between those present becomes destructive to the purpose of the case conference and she will have to ensure that any necessary decisions are taken.

We can identify a number of other principles which are central to the case conference. *The fact that a case conference is to be held, as well as its purpose, should always be explained to the service user.* It should be seen as a formal opportunity to review current and previous activity and actions and to make recommendations about future services required, and what will be necessary for any plans to be realized.

Service users should attend their case conferences and invitations to their family must be discussed with them. There will be occasions when making decisions in this area is difficult. The fact that, for various reasons, a user is unable to make decisions for herself should not in itself mean that she is wilfully excluded or her rights denied, nor that decision-making is assumed by others.

The frequency and format of case conferences should be made known to all involved. Who is to be invited? What questions will be asked of whom? What power and authority does the conference have? These are all questions which might cause users to feel anxious. Ideally such issues will have been worked through with users in anticipation of the case conference. Agreed set formats and frequency will obviously be helpful in this.

Adequate recording of the case conference is essential and should include a summary of all recommendations made. Such minutes should be circulated to all involved no later than two weeks after the conference. So often case conference decisions and discussions go unrecorded, which leaves the situation open to individual interpretation. The purpose of recording is to provide a record and to inform others; it also draws attention to resource needs and actions, and can provide a focus for supervision.

Some notes on preparation. A major purpose of case conferences is to plan and to review. It is important, therefore, that participants use the knowledge of a forthcoming case conference to prepare their contribution. We are not suggesting members have the event sewn up, but rather that possibilities are properly explored and user needs assessed in order to make appropriate recommendations. It is clearly unacceptable for the case conference to be used as an unstructured brainstorming session. One way to overcome this is to expect that all of the workers involved prepare, and ideally circulate, a brief report before the meeting.

The case conference proper. It may be useful to think of case conferences moving through the following stages: first, identifying needs; second, making plans; third, deciding on the review process. Though it will undoubtedly be rare for a case conference to move through these stages in a neat, sequential fashion, it should be the role of the chairperson to make sure that each stage has been considered. The review phase serves as a reminder that the case conference decision is a beginning and not an end.

Used effectively, case conferences can help to provide the necessary structure to ensure that users are actively involved in the planning process. They offer the potential for oversight and for consistent and coordinated effort to provide services.

Activity

Think back to a case conference you have attended. Try using the headings below to analyse the extent of its effectiveness.

- **Identifying need(s);**
- **Making plans;**
- **Deciding on review mechanisms.**

Working with relatives and volunteers

There are of course dilemmas for managers in encouraging the involvement of relatives and volunteers. There are a number of areas which need to be handled with sensitivity. Naturally the manager's task in working with relatives of users will vary according to the service group and the precise setting. At its most extreme, the manager's role may be to *prevent* users having contact with relatives who are considered to prejudice the user's interests. In the majority of cases, however, the manager will be attempting to *promote* a more cooperative approach to working with relatives.

Relatives may live in the locality and have a network of contacts. Relatives witness and experience the work of the service and as such can be projectors of its image. In residential and day care establishments, for example, relatives can provide stimulation and continuity for users. They may befriend them and form relationships. Working with relatives in this way can often be made part of the care plan for the user.

Clearly, then, relatives can provide for the user as well as make demands on the staff. In developing such relationships the following suggestions may be helpful:

- Encourage relatives and make them welcome. In residential and day care settings, can users or relatives make a drink? Are there strictly enforced visiting times? Remember images and credibility are generated by these contacts.
- Ensure that the responsibility for an open and friendly approach extends to all staff.
- Communicate freely, within the limitations of confidentiality. Relatives will make judgements based on the information they have. Confidence and trust can only come from being open and honest.
- Involve relatives fully in discussions and decisions about a user, including case conferences, reviews and planning.
- Make use of offers of help. Relatives, as outsiders, can bring different expertise and may usefully challenge practices.

Activity (if relevant)

Think about your current practice with relatives. Are there any points at which it could be improved? Try to be specific.

An expectation often placed on social care managers is the use of volunteers as a self-evidently 'good thing'. Our experiences would cause us to question this view and a blanket approach to its implementation as policy. The issue of how, whether or when to use volunteers is a complex one which is dependent on users, the staff group and the nature of the service provision. It may be tempting to see the use of volunteers as a helpful addition to staff when there are some tasks and activities which seem out of reach through lack of time or resources, but staff need to be reassured that volunteers will not take from them the activities which are peripheral to the caring task, but which they value or enjoy. On the other hand, volunteers need to feel that their contribution is necessary and valued. There are potential dilemmas in seeking to respond to these differing needs. Wherever possible, the manager has a responsibility to reconcile these needs in a constructive manner. It is important to work out, preferably as a full staff team, a stance towards volunteers, which forms the basis of a statement which can be updated and amended at regular intervals.

Such a statement might include:

- the purpose of working with volunteers at a particular point in time;
- the specific tasks considered suitable for volunteers, and some guidance on the ways in which they might be undertaken;
- a designated member of staff with responsibility for the deployment and supervision of volunteers;
- an acknowledgement of the needs of volunteers.

There can be little doubt that individual volunteering which evolves from contacts in a natural way is likely to lead to more sustained and durable relationships, with clearer benefits for individual clients. This approach is certainly preferable.

Activity

Think about your current practice with volunteers. Are there any points at which it could be improved? Try to be specific.

Managing your manager

Managers do not just manage other people: they are managed themselves. The mere mention of your manager is likely to conjure up a set of images! We suggest that you work through the following list in order to produce an all-round description of your relationship with your manager. Circle the numbers on the scales which you feel most clearly describe the relationship.

Does not keep me in the picture.	1	2	3	4	5	6	7	Keeps me in the picture.
Has vague or ambiguous objectives.	1	2	3	4	5	6	7	Has clear objectives.
Refuses to listen to my views.	1	2	3	4	5	6	7	Is prepared to listen to my views.
Not interested in my development.	1	2	3	4	5	6	7	Interested in my development.
Inconsistent in her policies.	1	2	3	4	5	6	7	Consistent in her policies.
Fails to represent my views.	1	2	3	4	5	6	7	Represents my views.

Unprepared to take decisions.	1	2	3	4	5	6	7	Prepared to take decisions.
Cannot count on her support.	1	2	3	4	5	6	7	Can count on her support.
Interferes in my work.	1	2	3	4	5	6	7	Does not interfere in my work.
Not available to see me.	1	2	3	4	5	6	7	Available to see me.
Takes credit herself for my contribution.	1	2	3	4	5	6	7	Gives credit to my contribution.
Unable to respect her.	1	2	3	4	5	6	7	Able to respect her.
Does not take an interest in my work.	1	2	3	4	5	6	7	Takes an interest in my work.
Overloads me with work.	1	2	3	4	5	6	7	Does not overload me.
Fails to provide opportunities and challenges.	1	2	3	4	5	6	7	Provides opportunities and challenges.

Now total the score (105 is the maximum). Does the score reflect your experience of the relationship?

In dealing with your manager it is possible to become passive, to succumb to being managed. We want to suggest that you develop an active approach to managing your manager. Managing your manager is part of your management role. We offer some suggestions of ways in which managing your manager can be improved.

Relate to your manager's world

Try to understand your manager's role, problems and needs and help her to achieve her aims. Recognize that she is dependent on you, as much as you are dependent on her. Don't abuse her time. Give her feedback and encourage her to do the same. Keep your manager informed; enable her to be supportive to you by not being caught out. If your manager is to work well for you she needs to understand your objectives and methods.

Promote respect

If you can gain your manager's respect, you will probably be given more autonomy. You do not have to sit and wait for the manager to respect you, you can promote respect:

- Be punctual for meetings.
- Be prepared with relevant documents.
- Ensure reports are on time.
- Anticipate jobs and undertake them without being asked.
- When you meet your manager, have a relevant agenda to ask/ tell about.
- Listen actively/take notes.

Some tactics

There may be times when other tactics are needed! Cultivate areas in which you are happy for your manager to intervene. These can be areas in which you welcome challenges which may help you to develop or refine your own thinking. They may be areas which enable you to engage your manager in issues directly pertinent to areas of work you need to test out or clarify or on which you need to seek common ground. If there *have* to be battles, always choose battlegrounds carefully. In such circumstances, ask for consistency and clarify what you expect the manager to do.

Managing meetings with other managers

As a manager you will spend time in meetings with other managers. These meetings may play a formative role in the development of policies which you can influence and will probably have to implement.

If a meeting with other managers has not gone well it is easy to identify things to criticize, such as an unsuitable room, an incompetent chairperson. As a participant in a meeting it is often difficult to be as critical about one's own performance in achieving and maintaining the meeting's effectiveness.

Activity

Think of the last meeting you attended with other managers, and try to answer the following questions:

1. **Overall did I influence the meeting positively or negatively? (Give examples.)**
2. **Did I prepare for the meeting?**
3. **Did I talk too much or too little?**
4. **Did I listen to other views?**

Answering these four simple questions can be revealing! In general terms a good contributor to a meeting with other managers is one who makes it easy for the chairperson to be a good chairperson. In practice this means preparation, by reading material relevant to the meeting and collecting your thoughts on it, perhaps making a few notes. It also means being ready to make contributions at the meeting itself which build on the suggestions of others as well as your own. In what areas do you need to improve your performance in meetings with other managers?

In conclusion, in the management of external links:

- Be clear   – about what each expects of the other.
- Be demanding – set high standards for yourselves and others.
- Be supportive – relationships need to be reciprocal.

7   Managing to train

How to read this chapter . . .
*   This chapter is about the manager's training role. It has three*
sections: identifying training needs, induction training and super-
vision. Each section can be read separately if you have an interest
in the topic it covers, or you can read the chapter as a whole if you
want a more rounded treatment of the manager's training role.

Introduction

As a manager, it is tempting to put training on the back burner;
to regard training as something that can be left until there is a
period of time when there is nothing more important to do.
    With the development of a system of National Vocational Quali-
fications (NVQ) in Social Care, the manager's training responsibilities are more sharply defined. NVQ requires managers to substantially reappraise their training roles, particularly in relation to the
assessment of staff's competence in the workplace. Much of your
time is spent working through other staff, as a resource to meet
service users' needs. If you take this feature of your work seriously,
staff training cannot be a low priority. Outside courses have a part
to play in staff training, but the manager's own training role is
paramount. After all, your grasp of what is required in a staff
member's job will be much more detailed than that of an outsider

and you will know individual members of staff's strengths and weaknesses.

In social care great stress is placed on the value of experience as a teacher, and this value cannot be denied. However this argument can be used as a rationalization for not providing training opportunities. There are sound reasons for the manager's involvement in training.

Firstly, if training is not provided, mistakes will occur which would otherwise have been avoided. Secondly, staff will be under-utilized if they are not trained. The delegation advocated in Chapter 2 depends to a large extent on adequate staff training. Thirdly, training may motivate staff if they perceive the possibility of enhanced job satisfaction and/or an improvement in their career prospects.

There are at least three areas of training which are the responsibility of the manager: identifying training needs, induction training and providing supervision.

Identifying training needs

Carrying out your continuing training role involves more than the *ad hoc* nomination of staff for external courses. The starting-point is to identify training needs, which itself begins by analysing the basic knowledge and skills required in each post and then refining them in the light of the potential contribution of individual staff members, according to their varying levels of performance. Further, identifying training needs must take account of personal interests and career aspirations. Once training needs have been identified they can be recorded on a training profile.

Activity

First of all, list the duties which are involved in the staff member's post. You can extract these from the job description, if there is one. If not, you will have to start from scratch. Then analyse the basic knowledge and skills required by the job. What would *anybody* doing this job need to know and be able to do? Insert this information on the profile, together with any training needs which emerge from it. Now modify this general analysis in the light of the individual staff member. Think about her level of performance. Does the staff member

**have training needs which are specific to her? Insert them in the
profile. Finally, include in the profile any specific training needs which
emerge out of the staff member's personal interests and career aspirations.**

TRAINING PROFILE

DUTIES	KNOWLEDGE	SKILLS	GENERAL TRAINING NEEDS	SPECIFIC TRAINING NEEDS	METHODS OF MEETING TRAINING NEEDS

A training profile can indicate to you the point each staff member
has reached in terms of her development, as well as the training
needs shared by a number of staff or the whole establishment. The
profile can help in identifying training which is necessary to improve
staff members' performance in their present posts and which will
aid their future development.

A training profile is an account of the knowledge and skills
required by each staff member in each aspect of her job, which
distinguishes the knowledge and skills on which to focus training
inputs. A profile could be used with each member of staff to
evaluate strengths and weaknesses in relation to each area of knowledge and skill. The construction of the profile should involve staff
members as fully as possible. Having constructed the training profile, you will have a list of the training needs of individual staff
members. These needs can be met in different ways. There may
be needs common to all staff which need to be tackled by using
the establishment's own resources and/or by bringing in outside
help. There may be areas in which only some staff have training
needs. These can be remedied by help from staff who are regarded
as competent, bearing in mind who can work with whom, or by
using an external course or supervision.

Induction training

In providing induction training the manager is introducing the new
staff member to her responsibilities and identifying where she can

find the support she requires. Of course, a new staff member cannot absorb everything at once. It is important to avoid giving her too much information at the outset, so it needs to be put into priority order. For example, in a large residential establishment:

1. By the end of the first week – conditions of service, trade union membership, Health and Safety. Fire drill.
2. By the end of the first month – familiarity with the work of her group/unit.
3. By the end of three months – familiarity with the work of the establishment as a whole.

As a manager you will need to work out your induction training according to the size of the service for which you are responsible and in such a way that it dovetails with any general arrangements which may exist for induction into the wider organization. If general arrangements do exist, they do not absolve the manager from the responsibility for induction training: supplement them as necessary.

Before the first meeting with the new member of staff, make sure that you have planned the whole of the first day. Ensure that she can be introduced to other staff and that arrangements are made to put her on the rota with the same person for the first few days. At the first meeting take things slowly. Remember what is routine and commonplace to you may be incomprehensible to her! Give out a written list of staff and clients, with their locations, if appropriate. In your desire to instil information, do not forget to ask whether she has any problems. In subsequent meetings, work through the philosophy and practice of the service. This will provide a good foundation for subsequent supervision. (For a detailed consideration of induction training see Douglas and Payne, 1988).

Supervision

Supervision is the main area in which a manager exercises her responsibility for training. As well as providing a manager with a system of accountability and members of staff with a means of support, supervision can have a training function which is concerned with the staff member's development. The training function of supervision recognizes the need for staff to have the basic knowledge and skills to carry out the job and to have the opportunity for further development of their potential. It involves learning from the job, in close proximity to it. It bridges the gap between learning and work. Supervision draws the learning out of work in a way which is consistent with what we know about the way adults learn by reflecting on real-life issues. Such an approach underpins the framework provided by NVQ (see Kelly *et al.* 1990, Section 3).

The traditional separation of training from work has created problems in applying knowledge gained from courses back at the workplace. It is futile to send staff on training courses to learn philosophies or practise techniques, for example normalization, reality orientation, group living, risk-taking, (even supervision!) which are not supported by the manager when the staff member returns from the course. The halo effect from the course seems to wear off soon after returning to work. Even ideas aimed at overcoming this problem, such as having to undertake follow-up work on a project related to the course on return to work, will fail if the manager regards it as a trivial pursuit. Staff will, by and large, be guided in their work by what they think the manager values and will reward. The residential manager in an establishment for adults who has all the rhetoric about independent living, but who carries around a mental bath book, will usually have staff who understand that choice is less important than routine bathing, even if they too become fluent in the new vocabulary. Philosophy may be one thing, practice another. Managers need to accept this fact of life and to base their staff training on it, rather than ignoring it by trying to teach staff philosophies and techniques off-the-job which will remain a trainer's pipe-dream when the staff go back to work. Supervision is, therefore, one of the most powerful tools for staff training and development. All too frequently in social care management it is either regarded with suspicion – or it assumes the status of a buzz word. Managers may not be sure what is meant by supervision, so that much of what has been done has been instinctive, rather than deliberate and purposeful.

Supervision is essentially a simple concept. It is on-the-job staff training and development, with somebody asking questions and making observations which are probably, but not necessarily, drawn from greater expertise. It is regular feedback to the staff member on her performance. It is managers spending time in planning their efforts to help staff develop, using real-life situations as they occur. In social care, the word 'supervision' has often been used rather more narrowly, and been equated with surveillance. Supervision is not a question of the manager checking up on staff from time to time and putting them right. Nor is it the patronizing passing on of hard-won experience and throwing in a lecture to be absolutely sure the message has gone home! It is much more a question of making the member of staff aware of how she performs in her job, of making her think about it, and of encouraging her to try new approaches as opportunities present themselves. It is important for the manager to convey to a staff member that supervision is *her* time. This can be demonstrated by the manager's commitment to regular and uninterrupted supervision sessions. The range of activities regarded as supervision can be wide. It is not even confined to focusing on the staff member. It can be about the manager giving insight into her own job, showing the member of staff a broader view and admitting that there are problems to which the manager does not necessarily have an answer: for example, when discussing a forthcoming case conference.

Any event or incident can be used as potential material for the purpose of supervision before, during and after its occurrence. Some situations hold more possibilities for staff training than others. The basic approach is to focus on the potential for learning, rather than giving instructions.

Activity

What sort of incidents offer the potential for supervision in your work setting? Your list might include incidents relating to the following:

- **admission,**
- **participating in a case conference,**
- **discharge,**
- **presenting an item at a staff meeting,**
- **death of a service user,**
- **mistakes,**
- **changes in policies.**

An immediate response to the sort of approach to supervision which we have outlined could be either that it is quicker to do things yourself or that it is easier to tell staff what to do. This response can disguise a reluctance to let go and allow staff to assume more responsibility, which may require considerable courage in allowing mistakes to be made, providing that they do not jeopardize users' quality of life. Afterwards, mistakes can be pursued in supervision. What has the member of staff learned? How could things have been done differently? Were the staff member's assumptions wrong? In what other circumstances has the staff member employed the same assumptions?

We have suggested that any incident is an opportunity for supervision, but some times are better than others. Two days after a big mistake might be better than one hour later! It is important to make time before predictable important events, for example the staff member who is conducting her first admission to a day care centre or making her first presentation at a case conference, and to review how well it went afterwards. Important events can be opportunities which are lost, unless they are dwelt on while they are fresh in the member of staff's mind. Finally, the ready availability of *ad hoc* supervision opportunities in many social care settings should not obscure the need for planned supervision sessions.

We want to demystify supervision, by suggesting a few basic principles:

- If you have to criticize, try to do it without crushing the person. Allow the member of staff to save face; point out her strengths and so on.

- Choose realistic goals in areas in which you are trying to improve the staff member's performance. There is no point in trying to tackle areas which the member of staff will not change at any cost. Concentrate on strengths as much as training needs.

- Try to select issues which, if resolved, will have a marked effect.

- Ask questions, rather than giving instructions. The aim is self-development, not telling the person everything you know! Provoke alternative thoughts – what else could you have done? What would change your mind?

- Keep a brief record of the main issues covered, any decisions made and work to be undertaken before the next session.

The will to supervise is just as important as sophisticated techniques. It is the most effective form of staff training and development. It acknowledges the influence of the manager on staff and it is without the problems of transferring learning from a course, as when having to demonstrate relevance. Effective supervision increases the confidence and broadens the perspective of staff.

8 Managing to care: standards, quality and change

How to read this chapter . . .
    This chapter reminds the reader that the purpose of management is to ensure that a service provides effectively for its users. The chapter can thus be seen as the culmination of consideration of specific aspects of the management role in the manager's overall responsibility for quality assurance and managing change. Some readers may want to use the final part of the chapter, on managing change, in conjunction with material from other chapters if they are contemplating specific initiatives as a result of earlier reading.

Managing to care: standards and quality

Social care, at its best, will be considerably more than a response to basic needs such as food, warmth and security. High quality care, which is able to respond to varied individual needs, does not just happen – it has to be *planned*. In planning to provide care, the manager has a particular responsibility for setting standards against which can be judged the quality of care provided by a particular service. Standards are only of use if they are used to assess the services provided. Even the most sophisticated set of standards will be empty rhetorical statements unless they are put to use. In developing a strategy for quality assurance, therefore, standards are the foundation.

The Social Services Inspectorate has suggested three overlapping areas in which standards need to be set:

1. Quality of life: the benefits to consumers;
2. Quality of care: the quality of resources and activities in the process of providing care;
3. Quality of management: the extent to which the activities of managers contribute to meeting agreed objectives.

(Social Services Inspectorate 1990, p. 6.)

Standards have to be set for social care services which are very varied and which are intended to meet different combinations of needs, for instance, for

●   people who are vulnerable, frail or confused;
●   people who have emotional and/or behavioural difficulties;
●   people with disabilities; and
●   people who have experienced a range of social and economic disadvantages.

As a consequence, management structures and styles have to vary to match these differences in the users served, and the different tasks to be performed. An example of this is the need to ensure that services respond to racial inequalities and cultural diversity (SCA, 1990). Another example concerns the extent to which systems are open and democratic, with the intention of fully involving users, whilst others may be geared primarily to the delivery of personal care. There are then many forces which will affect the development of quality services. For example in a residential establishment the total group consists of residents and staff. As group members, each have particular roles to play in making a contribution to the dynamics of the community. Like staff, residents can contribute to the running of an establishment. Like residents, staff also have needs. Nevertheless residents use an establishment because of their needs and staff work in an establishment to help meet those needs. Staff are paid for their work and are accountable for it. The manager is responsible for effectively managing these and many other aspects of the service within social care settings. A complex range of interactions and interests have to be balanced in ways which contribute to the 'quality of life' of users.

Activity

Make a list of the factors which affect your ability to provide *quality* services. First, you may find it easier to generate a negative list of factors which are not conducive to quality services such as:

- poor communication
- poor procedures
- poor judgement
- carelessness

Now move on and try to make a positive list. This will probably include many of the issues which this book has identified as important aspects of a manager's role. Our list is not exhaustive but rather is intended to illustrate the main factors which affect the delivery of a quality service:

- policies
- clear and agreed aims and objectives
- guidance and procedures
- codes of practice; staff handbooks
- service organisation
- attitudes and values
- competence of the staff
- training
- supervision and support
- good communication
- consistency in approach.

Of course, in developing a quality service the manager does not operate in a vacuum. The overall *policies* of the service as determined by the agency – whether it is in the statutory, private or voluntary sector – are important determinants. They will shape the context of the manager's role. However, the manager should ideally have some input into the formulation of policy based on practice experiences. These policies should lead to the setting of *clear aims and objectives* which make explicit the values which underpin the service and the intended outcomes. It is important that the aims and objectives of a service are available for all to see, and that staff and, if possible, users have an opportunity to contribute to any necessary changes in the formulation of the objectives. Such a statement of objectives will lead on to more detailed information about the running of the service, *guidance and procedures*, and from this should follow job descriptions for all staff.

The agency's policies are, therefore, only the starting point for developing quality services. In order to direct systematic attention to the meeting of needs, effective management is likely to start with statements which seek to translate policies into practice objectives which lead to procedures (ideally mutually agreed by users and staff members) which are likely to cover the following areas:

- referral criteria
- staffing requirements and staff selection
- working methods
- meetings
- supervision structure
- mechanisms for decision-making
- resource implications
- management structure and style.

This list is intended to give an indication of the range of activities which require planned procedures by managers pursuing quality. The purpose of drawing up such procedures is to make clear statements about what policies mean in terms of day-to-day practice.

The process is obviously a dynamic one and should not be seen as simply a case of dictating tasks and working methods. It has to be understood by all staff and worked on by all staff and ideally users. It will constantly require up-dating and amending as the tasks, the users and the staff group change. It will be important for managers to ensure that the elements listed above are co-ordinated and channelled towards effective care.

A systematic approach of this kind to the management of care obviously needs to be worked through in each particular service. For example, no two residential establishments, groups of users or teams of staff will be the same, even in services sharing broad aims and similar working methods.

Shifts in social policy which require statutory agencies to move from being providers to enablers with a greater emphasis on the development of partnerships (Department of Health 1989) will require greater skills of managers wherever they are located. Implicit in these developments is greater autonomy and more responsibility for front-line managers in social care settings. In addition, the competence-based approach to training of N.V.Q. will require clearly defined aims and objectives and an infrastructure of supervision (Kelly et al, 1990). These developments reinforce the value of setting services in a quality assurance framework of the kind set out by Payne (1989, p.41).

Development of user
responsive agency
For Staff ◄─────────── policies and strategies ─────► For Clients

| Issues of codes/ guidelines of 'good practice'; establishment of standards and expectations. | Provision of information and services to users enabling informed choices to be made. |

↓   ↓

| Development of monitoring, evaluation and inspection systems; including criteria and indicators of achievement of 'good practice'. 'User feedback' obtained. | Availability of information on individual homes. Statements of philosophy and objectives. |

↓   ↓

| | Charter of rights and contract. |

↓

| Development of effective management, staff supervision, development and training. | Obligation of resident/client to contribute to quality assurance by respecting rights of other residents. |

↓   ↓

| Constructing a regime that gives privacy, choice and security to residents. | Consumer views of quality of life in home. |

'Star' ratings for
homes as certified by
independent assessors.

Figure 8.1   Elements of a quality assurance strategy

Managing change

The implication of much of what we have discussed in this chapter and elsewhere is that, for many managers, the issue of managing change looms large. Some managers may have waited years to be in a position which enables them to exercise more influence and they may relish the opportunity to make changes which they regard as important. Other managers may have been appointed with a specific brief from higher management to 'shake things up' or 'sort things out'. Some managers may be eagerly awaited by staff and service users, in anticipation that they will overturn regimes which have been detested. In any of these circumstances, the temptation is to want to make an impact quickly or even to succumb to change for change's sake. Unless there is an immediate crisis to be resolved, consider your actions carefully. Change can have far-reaching repercussions for individual users, the user group, individual staff, the staff group or the whole service. It is not necessarily the change itself which determines the repercussions, but the social implications of the change. An obvious example of this would be moving the furniture in a lounge in a residential establishment for older people. The disturbance brought about by change requires time for adjustments to be made. It may also require supportive activities, such as training.

The role of the social care manager is increasingly concerned with the management of change. This may be in terms of changing service organization and delivery, or staff responsibilities and deployment. In anticipating the introduction of change it is useful to reflect on the framework used by Plant (1987):

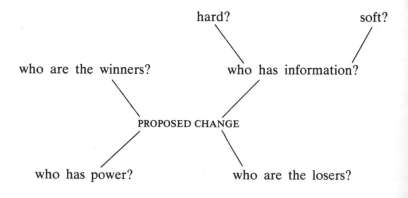

This simple framework can be used for any change which is being considered. The questions enable the manager to identify support as well as opposition, points of consensus and possible conflict. This information should provide pointers for future work.

Who has information? Hard or soft?

It is important for the detailed planning of the change process to have access to information which informs developments. Effective communication is essential. Hard information is likely to include detailed statistical data on, for example, budgets, demand for services and aspects of the organization such as staffing and future plans. Soft information relates to knowledge of a team or service which enables an understanding of where a team is in terms of development, what are considered sensitive issues, as well as aspects of reliability, support and previous achievements and successes. Both hard and soft information can be very helpful in determining the most appropriate and effective strategies for the introduction of change. Often hard information is available but not translated into usable forms and soft information is carried around unconsciously by managers and only used intuitively.

Who has power?

All managers recognize that it is not simply those with position, authority and status in the formal structure of organizations who have power. In many social care establishments power is vested in others who occupy positions much lower in the formal hierarchy, such as a long-serving cook or domestic, a popular care assistant, a member of staff who is a trade union representative. Identifying those with informal power and influence is likely to be critical to the introduction of change within teams and services. It is worth acknowledging that in some settings informal power may rest with service users and, in any case, being aware of their needs during change is paramount.

A consideration of these questions leads on to asking 'Who are winners?' and 'Who are losers?' The identification of informal leaders and opinion-shapers needs to relate to this. Those considered 'winners' are obviously more likely to be supportive of any change proposals. Having identified aspects of the system and staff group which fall into each camp, attention will need to be directed at recognizing the needs of each group and in making the 'losers' into 'winners'.

Plant's framework is a useful starting-point, but in bringing about complex changes, it is useful to work systematically through a series of stages:

ANALYSIS OF THE BACKGROUND	to the change contemplated
STRATEGY	for bringing about the change
IMPLEMENTATION	of the change
REACTIONS	to the change
RESPONSE	to the reactions
FOLLOW-UP	

(Lewin, 1951, and Pfeiffer and Jones, 1974)

We suggest that you work through these stages in thinking about a change in which you are engaged or which you are contemplating or which you have already implemented. (*Note*   What follows is written in the present tense, but can be used to analyse past experiences or to think about possible changes in the future.)

The management of change is an appropriate point at which to end. The initial chapter introduced the wider context of changes within which social care has had to operate and the ways in which these changes have shaped the development of services. This final chapter has highlighted the central message of the book, namely that it is all too easy for managers to succumb to dealing with a series of separate events, simply reacting day by day, hour by hour, minute by minute to what is happening to them. In relation to managing change, as with so many of the topics covered in this book, a manager needs to be able to collect information, to plan and to implement her plan. Although much of such activity is the stuff of good social care practice in face-to-face work with service users, we would be ill-advised to assume that managers are able automatically to utilize these skills when they move on to management.

For those people who have moved on to social care management or who are contemplating such a move, this book has been intended as a modest contribution to the process of adapting such skills.

Stages in the process of managing change

Analysis of the background to change

The problem is:

The change(s) I wish to bring about is (are):

Some questions to help you analyse why you are contemplating change and the nature of the change which is likely to result are as follows:

1. How important is the problem which is prompting change?
2. Is the problem recognised by anyone else?
3. Is there agreement on the need for change and the areas in which it ought to take place?
4. What level of trust exists?
5. Do those affected by the change have previous experience of change? If so, how is their previous experience likely to affect them?
6. Does the change contemplated threaten particular roles or statuses, the balance of power, values, attitudes?

Strategy for bringing about change

After answering the questions in the previous section, you should possess sufficient information about the forces acting for and against change to formulate a strategy for bringing change about, initially by concentrating on actions which will *increase* the forces for change and *decrease* the forces against change.

Forces for change   *Actions to increase*

1.

2.

3.

4.

5.

6.

Forces against change   *Actions to decrease*

1.

2.

3.

4.

5.

6.

Strategy – Detailed Action Plan

For each of the actions you have identified as necessary, set out
your objectives, timescale, resources required and whose support
you need to win in order to carry out each action:

Action necessary : Objectives : Timescale : Resources : Support :

Implementation of change

1. In implementing the change, is it best to introduce it all at
    once, or in stages?
2. Is it advisable to describe it as something new or as an extension
    of current policy and/or practice?
3. How will it be presented? (Written/verbal report, at a meeting,
    on the noticeboard?)

(Anticipated) reactions to change

You will already have a good idea of the extent to which the change will be welcomed or resisted from your work so far.

1. Will it be accepted? (Passively, guardedly, enthusiastically?)
2. Will it be resisted? (Inaction, adherence to present values, fear, not feasible?)
3. Will resistance or acceptance occur initially, at a later stage, continuously?
4. How will this change affect you?

(Anticipated) response to the reactions:

When you are faced with the reactions to the change, you need to be clear about your stance in respect of other points of view and the extent to which you are prepared to make modifications in response to the reactions. To what extent:

1. Will you work with the sources of resistance? (Make proposals for modifications, give reassurance, engage in conflict?)
2. Will you work with the sources of acceptance? (Engage them in implementation/modification, delegate, try to hold back counter-productive enthusiasm?)

Follow-up

Before you breathe a sigh of relief, remember that you may learn a good deal from following up the change.

1. What is the outcome? (Not implemented, waiting period before implementation, partial implementation, full implementation and effective in resolving problem, full implementation but not effective in resolving problem.)
2. If the outcome is successful, can you expect continued support for the change or fresh difficulties?

Bibliography

Two of the most influential books about management in general published in recent years are:

Peters, T.J. and R.H. Waterman (1982) *In Search of Excellence* (Harper & Row, New York).
Peters, T. (1987) *Thriving on Chaos* (Macmillan, London).

Two British books in similar vein are:

Goldsmith, W. and D. Clutterbuck (1984) *The Winning Streak* (Weidenfeld & Nicolson, London).
Hickman, C.R. and M.A. Silva (1984) *Creating Excellence* (George Allen & Unwin, London).

The remainder of the bibliography gives the references cited in individual chapters, plus additional references for readers who wish to study particular issues in more detail.

Chapter 1

Audit Commission (1986) *Making a Reality of Community Care* (HMSO, London).
Barclay Report (1982) *Social Workers: Their Role and Tasks* (Bedford Square Press, London).
Department of Health (1989) White Paper *Caring for People.* (HMSO, London).
Department of Health (1990) *Management Development: Guidance*

for Local Authority Social Services Departments (Social Services Inspectorate).

Drucker, P. (1975) *The Practice of Management* (Pan, London).

Goffman, G (1968) *Asylums* (Pelican, Harmondsworth).

Griffiths Report (1988) *Community Care: An Agenda for Action* (HMSO, London).

Lane, D. (ed.) (1984) *Beyond Barclay: The Future of Residential Care* (Social Care Association, Surbiton).

Lane, D. (ed.) (1984) *The Bonington Report. Residential Services: The Next Ten Years* (Social Care Association, Surbiton).

Lawrence, P. (1986) *Invitation to Management* (Blackwell, Oxford).

Mount, A. (1977) *The Rise and Fall of the British Manager* (Macmillan, London).

Parker, R.A. (1988) 'An Historical Background to Residential Care', in I. Sinclar (ed.), *Residential Care: The Research Reviewed* (Wagner Report, Vol. 2) (HMSO, London).

Philpot, T. (ed.) (1982) *A New Direction for Social Work? The Barclay Report and Its Implications* (Community Care/IPC Business Press).

Philpot, T. (ed.) (1984) *Group Care Practice: The Challenge of the Next Decade* (Community Care/Business Press International).

Social Care Association (1990) *Action Checklist for Anti-Racist Practice in Social Care* (Surbiton).

Wagner Report (1988) *Residential Care: A Positive Choice* (HMSO, London).

Chapter 2

Barrett, F.D. (1977) 'Perspectives on Time Management', *Management by Objectives*, 6(1), pp. 37–45.

Boydell, T. and M. Pedler (eds.) (1981) *Management Self-Development* (Gower, Aldershot).

Bryman, A. (1986) *Leadership and Organisations* (Routledge & Kegan Paul, London).

Carlson, S. (1951) *Executive Behaviour* (Stromberg, Stockholm).

Cranwell-Ward, J. (1988) *Managing Stress* (Gower, Aldershot).

McDerment, L. (1988) *Stress in Residential and Day Care* (Social Care Association, Surbiton).

McGregor, D. (1960) *The Human Side of Enterprise* (McGraw-Hill, New York).

Mackenzie, R.A. (1972) *The Time Trap: How to Get More Done in Less Time* (McGraw-Hill, New York).

Mintzberg, H. (1973) *The Nature of Managerial Work* (Harper & Row, New York).

Pedler, M., J. Burgoyne and T. Baychell (1978) *A Manager's Guide to Self-Development* (McGraw-Hill, New York).

Peters, T.J. and R.H. Waterman (1982) *In Search of Excellence* (Harper & Row, New York).

Sayles, L.R. (1979) *Leadership: What Effective Managers Really Do and How They Do It* (McGraw-Hill, New York).

Scott, J. and A. Rochester (1984) *Effective Management Skills: Managing People* (Sphere/British Institute of Management).

Social Services Inspectorate (1988) *Managing to Care. A study of First Line Managers in Social Services Departments in Day and Domiciliary Care* (Department of Health, London).

Chapter 3

Avery, R.D. and J.E. Campion (1982) 'The Employment Interview: A Summary and Review of Recent Research', *Personal Psychology*, 35, pp. 281–322.

De Board, R. (1983) *Counselling People at Work: An Introduction for Managers* (Gower, Aldershot).

Goodworth, C. (1987) *Effective Interviewing: How to Get the Right Person for the Job* (Century Hutchinson, London).

Hachett, P. (1978) *Interview Skills Training. Role Play Exercises* (Institute of Personnel Management, London).

Higham, M. (1979) *The ABC of Interviewing* (Institute of Personnel Management, London).

Kahan, B., G. Banner and D. Lane (1986) *Staff . . . Finding Them, Choosing Them, Keeping Them* (Social Care Association, Surbiton).

Rae, L. (1988) *The Skills of Interviewing* (Gower, Aldershot).

Chapter 4

Adair, J. (1987) *Effective Team Building* (Pan, London).

Belbin, M.R. (1981) *Management Teams: Why They Succeed or Fail* (Heinemann, London).

Brown, A (1986) *Groupwork* (Gower, Aldershot).

Brown, A and R. Clough (eds) (1989) *Groups and Groupings. Life and Work in Day and Residential Centres* (Tavistock/Routledge, London).

Elgood, C. (1984) *Handbook of Management Games* (Gower, Aldershot).

Harris, J. and S. Valentine (1982) 'Time Out for Team Practice: Structured Participation as a Method of Training for Team Maintenance and Development', *Social Work Education* 1(2), pp. 11–15.

Payne, C. and T. Scott (1982) *Developing Supervision of Teams in Field and Residential Social Work* (National Institute of Social Work, London).

Payne, M. (1982) *Working in Teams* (Macmillan, London).

Peel, M. (1988) *How to Make Meetings Work* (Kogan Page, London).

Tropman, J.E. (1980) *Effective Meetings* (Sage, London).

Tuckman, B.W. (1965) 'Developmental Sequences in Small Groups,' *Psychological Bulletin* 63(6).

Woodcock, M. (1979) *Team Development Manual* (Gower, Aldershot).

Chapter 5

Willcocks, P., S. Peace and L. Kellaher (1987) *Private Lives in Public Places* (Tavistock, London).

Chapter 6

Hastings, C., P. Bixby and R. Chaudhry-Lawton (1986) *The Superteam Solution* (Gower, Aldershot).

Kahan, B. (1987) 'United We Stand . . . ', *Social Services Insight*, (2 Oct. 87, pp. 18–19).

Kelly, D. (1988) 'Maximising Quality in the Residential Environment', *Social Work Today*, 4 Mar. 88, pp. 21–5.
SCA/BASW (1987) Policy Statement on Keyworking. (Social Care Association, Surbiton).

Chapter 7

Atherton, J. (1986) *Professional Supervision in Group Care* (Tavistock, London).
Payne, C. and T. Scott (1982) *Developing Supervision of Teams in Field and Residential Social Work. Parts I and II* (National Institute of Social Work, London).
Williams, B. (1977) *Communicating Effectively: A Manager's Guide to Getting Through to People* (Thomson, Wellingborough).
See section on video packages which follows bibliography.

Chapter 8

Centre for Policy on Ageing (1984) *Home Life: A Code of Practice for Residential Care* (London).
Clough, R. (1982) *Residential Work* (Macmillan, London).
Davis, L. (1982) *Residential Care: A Community Resource* (Heinemann, London).
Department of Health (1989) White Paper *Caring for People* (HMSO, London).
Drucker, P. (1981) *Managing in Turbulent Times* (Pan, London).
Hoggett, P. and V. Russell (1988) 'Organising for a Change', *Local Government Studies*, March, pp. 11–17.
Kelly, D., C. Payne and J. Warwick (1990) *Making National Vocational Qualifications Work for Social Care* (National Institute for Social Work and Social Care Association, London).
Lewin, K. (1951) *Field Theory in Social Science* (Harper & Row, New York).
Payne, C. (1989) *Better services for Older People* (National Institute of Social Work, London).
Pfeiffer, J.W. and J.E. Jones (1974) *A Handbook of Structured Experiences for Human Relations Training*, Vol. II, pp. 79–81, (University Associates, California).

Plant, R. (1987) *Managing Change and Making It Stick* (Gower, Aldershot).

Social Care Association (1990) *Action Checklist for Anti-Racist Practice in Social Care* (Surbiton).

Social Services Inspectorate (1989) *Homes are for Living In* (Department of Health, HMSO, London).

Social Services Inspectorate (1990) *Caring for Quality* (Department of Health, HMSO, London).

Work packs and video packages

Counselling at Work   Video and handbook produced by NACAB Vision with the help of Employee Advisory Resource.

Training for Care Home Managers   Pembroke Group, Video Arts and ESCATA.

Supervision and Management in Social Work   A package of three video tapes for front-line managers, produced by CCETSW.

Managing into the Future   ESCATA.

The Manager as Trainer   LGTB. A self-development package for managers of residential establishments and day care centres.

Training for Care: Training Material for Staff in Residential Homes for Elderly People   A package of workbooks with advice on how to run training sessions. LGTB.

In Search of Excellence; A Passion for Excellence   Video training packages based on the bestselling books of the same title by Peters and Waterman.

Manage Your Stress   A complete package including video developed by McGraw-Hill training systems and designed to be used in a workshop setting.

Could You be a Better Manager?   A set of LGTB workbooks which aim to help managers in local government identify their personal development needs and prepare a plan to meet them.

Domiciliary Care Managers' Workbook   An LGTB framework for new managers in this sector, which sets out the context within which they work.

Learning about Caring: An Introductory Package for Staff Development in Residential and Day Care Work   A set of materials enabling managers to organize training programmes for staff, NISW.

All Change (The Management of Change)   A Video Arts pro-
duction aimed at business but with some useful material for social
care managers.

When Can You Start? (Selection Techniques)   Video Arts pro-
duction working through the stages involved in recruitment and
selection.

Management and Action   An LGTB package developed specifically
for front-line managers in social services departments.

Index